~ La Chaire ~

~

The Story of Jersey's Lost Garden

~

Stephen Harmer M.A.

SEAFLOWER BOOKS
in association with
Hadlow College, Kent

Published in 2014 by
Seaflower Books in associatoion with
Hadlow College, Kent

Origination by Seaflower Books

www.ex-librisbooks.co.uk

Printed by CPI Antony Rowe
Chippenham, Wiltshire

ISBN 978-1-906641-75-7

I dedicate this book to Charles Fletcher who never lived long enough to enjoy what he had created.

Contents

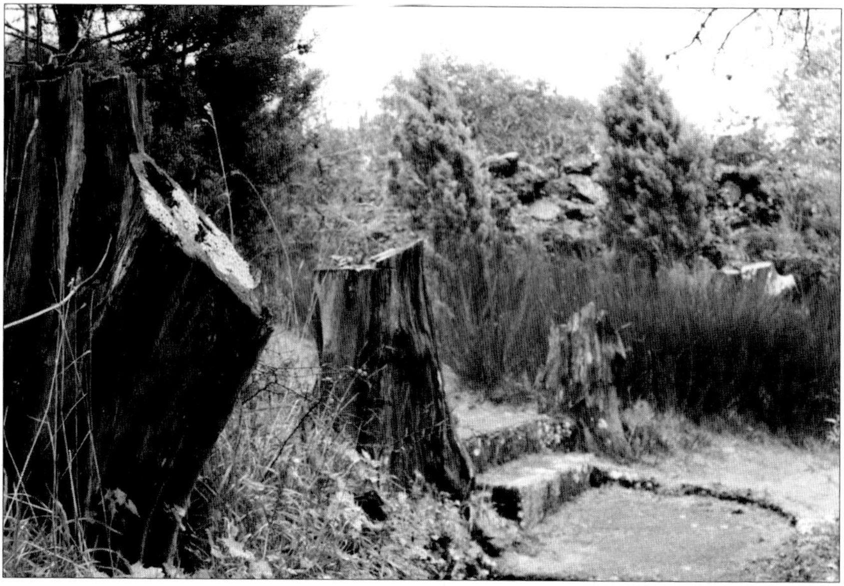

Fig 1 Part of the original shelter belt that was planted by Curtis in 1842. The trees in the photograph were considered dangerous and cut down in the late 1970s early 1980s by former owner John Brewster.

Introduction

The once well-known garden of La Chaire nestles in a sheltered valley on the north-east coast of Jersey near the former fishing village of Rozel. This book tells the story of its chequered history.

I have undertaken research among archival sources such as the Jersey Archive, the Société Jersiaise, and at the Archives of the Royal Botanic Gardens, Kew. Information has been gathered from interviews with people who remember La Chaire when it was still a garden and people with a current connection. In addition I have undertaken site analysis and investigation, including an exploration of the remains of the garden, in an effort to ascertain the position of the original features.

The story includes brief biographies of the two major figures, Samuel Curtis and Charles Fletcher, whose work has shaped the garden and demonstrates that La Chaire bears little or no resemblance to the original garden laid out by Curtis, but is the result of the infrastructural work completed by Fletcher. Curtis saw La Chaire as a garden capable of supporting the long-term survival of rare, tropical, and sub-tropical plants.

La Chaire today is a totally different place in comparison to its halcyon days from 1842 to 1906 during the tenure of Curtis and Fletcher, its two influential owners. The garden during this time displayed a wealth of rare and tropical plants that flourished in the comparatively temperate Jersey climate. The garden was protected behind a *Quercus ilex* and *Cupressus macrocarpa* shelter belt.

Today the south side of the valley at La Chaire is dark in places, narrowed and shaded by overgrown laurel, holly, ash and holm oak. Traces of past planting can still be seen, with bamboo, rhododendron and acacia. This is the residual planting from the Curtis, Fletcher, and later periods, that has now naturalised. Today the acacias are considered weeds by neighbours bordering the garden, and treated as an unwanted nuisance.

Terrace walls that were first commissioned for Curtis and then built upon and extended by Fletcher have to a large degree stood the test of time and the degradation caused by weather. The freeze/thaw effect is not as pronounced as in the UK due to the higher winter mean temperatures. This is influenced by the island only being four miles from north to south and the warm air off the sea being felt virtually island-wide, bar the very centre. The walls were constructed using a lime mix which is flexible and absorbs movement, so avoiding a destabilising effect and subsequent cracking. The paths have not survived so well and have been broken up and made uneven by tree roots and general wear caused by precipitation. The steps leading to each terrace are narrow and the tread-depth shallow, making them even more precarious in wet weather.

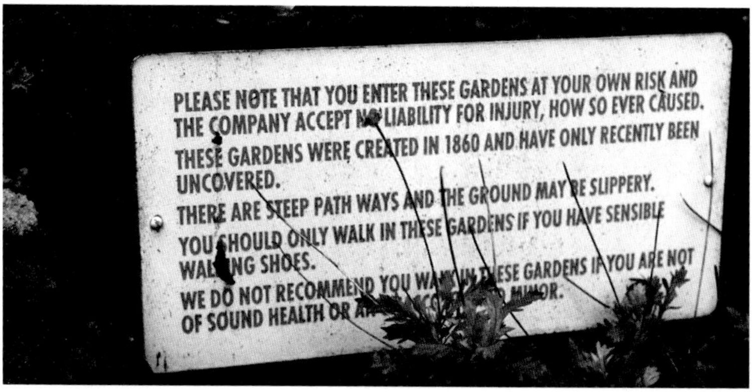

Fig 2 The signage at the entrance to the garden which lies behind Chateau La Chaire, now a hotel owned and run by the Hatton Hotel Group. The sign is incorrect; the garden was created from 1841. But it does allude to how precarious and dangerous the garden can be if not careful.

In winter the garden exudes a dark damp feeling of melancholy. This is not the atmosphere sought after in eighteenth century Rococo gardens, such as at Painshill with Charles Hamilton's Roman mausoleum, but a claustrophobic brooding effect.

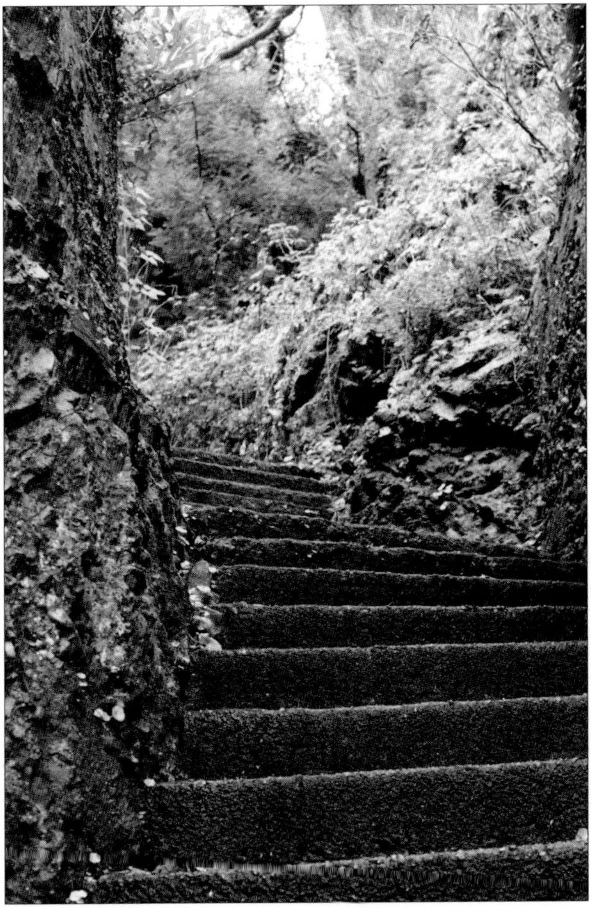

Fig 3 The feeling of melancholy is palpable along with a sense of decay as can be seen from these terrace steps on the south side

However, summer on the south side, behind the chateau, is different. Although the sun does not fully penetrate many areas of the garden, it does give an attractive dappled light and picturesque quality. The north side favoured by Curtis for his Himalayan plants and where he created walkways through rhododendron glades is now almost impenetrable. The native growth has taken over and long ago strangled the plants that he collected.

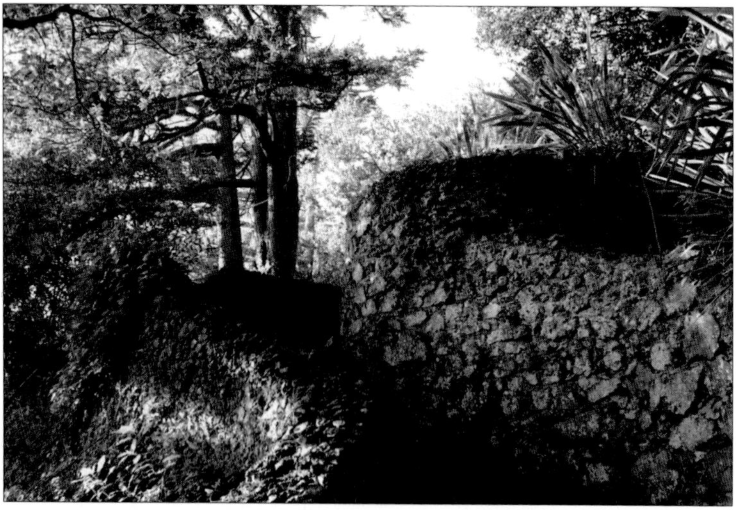

Fig 4 The photograph shows the garden today, a terrace directly behind the Chateau.

The Island of Jersey lies in the Bay of St Malo in the English Channel. The garden of La Chaire is on the north-east coast, on the easting WV694540 – see Fig 5 opposite which illustrates the north-east corner of Jersey and the location of the garden of La Chaire.

The history of La Chaire has never before been written about in any great detail, except for a few articles about the garden as well as about Samuel Curtis and Charles Fletcher. Some of the articles published have proved to be inaccurate.

Focus was directed towards La Chaire during 2004, when a 30-minute programme on BBC2 entitled *More Hidden Gardens* was presented by Chris Beardshaw. Its purpose was to draw attention to the proposed restoration of La Chaire, its creation by Samuel Curtis and the proposal to return the garden and the planting to the time of his tenure. The name Curtis was well-known in horticultural circles as a result of his connection with the *Botanical Magazine*, founded in 1787 by William Curtis, Samuel's father-in-law. A garden created by a Curtis would be a potential draw for botanists and interested members of the public. The programme repeatedly overlooked the fact that Charles

Fletcher, who purchased La Chaire in 1898, rebuilt the garden. He changed its appearance to the point that Curtis would have struggled to recognise what he had originally created. The influence of Fletcher had not, at this time, been fully researched or appreciated.

Fletcher was, and is still, unknown, and not therefore considered likely to entice the public to visit. Fletcher's name was also unlikely to persuade The States of Jersey to release the £3.5 million funding essential to restore La Chaire at that time.[1]

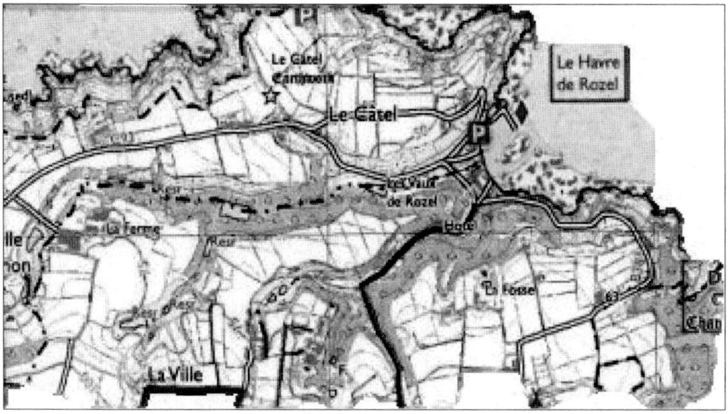

Fig 5 Section of official map of Jersey illustrating the north-east corner of the island and the location of the garden of La Chaire © States of Jersey

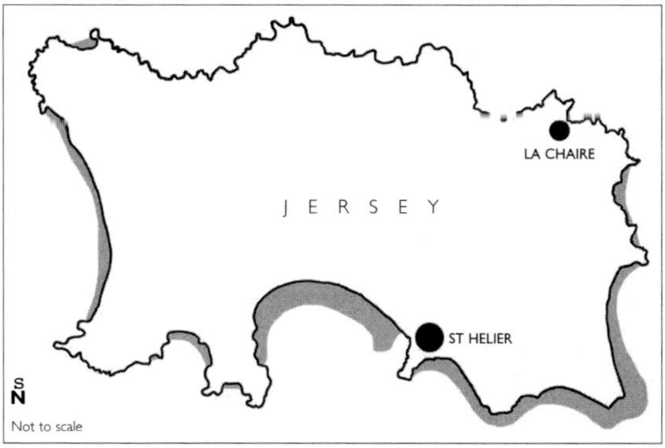

Fig 6 Map of Jersey showing the position of La Chaire and its geographical relation to the capital, St Helier

~ 1 ~

Samuel Curtis (1779-1860): The Making of a Plantsman

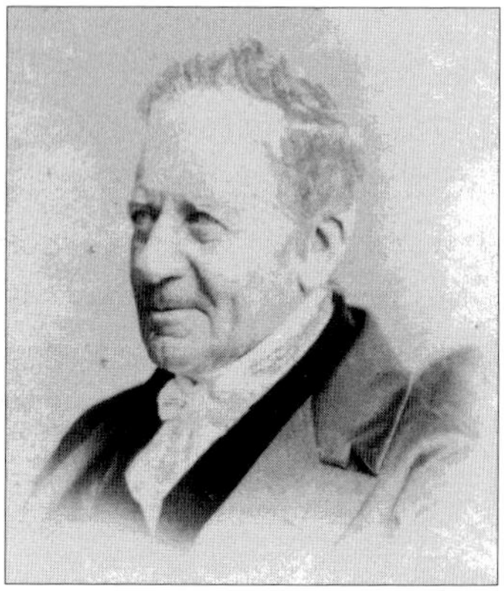

Samuel Curtis was the horticulturist and plantsman who designed, built and planted the first garden at La Chaire. It was laid out by Curtis and his widowed daughter Harriet Fothergill in 1841. La Chaire never belonged to him but was purchased by Harriet. Harriet bought the land from Thomas Machon which at that time was called Le Mont Crevieu ou Le Chaires.[2] Most likely after the death of her husband, Harriet decided to buy La Chaire and live with her father again as his companion.

Curtis was born on 29th August 1779, at Walworth, Surrey, to an established Quaker family. His great-grandfather, Thomas Curtis, held the Crown of Bohemia on his coat-of-arms which had been granted to his ancestor, Henry De Curteys. Thomas was a surgeon and apothecary as was James his son, the grandfather of Samuel Curtis. The family seat was at Alton in Hampshire, the house today being the family museum. Samuel was cousin to William Curtis who in 1777 published his first volume of *Flora Londinesis* and in 1787 published the first copy of the *Botanical Magazine*.

When William Curtis died, his wife and daughter Sarah inherited this publication. On 19th October, 1801, Samuel married Sarah who was then 19. They were married at Newington Church in London. Samuel and Sarah had a happy 26-year marriage, producing 13 children – eight girls and five boys. There are unsubstantiated claims that Samuel Curtis was engaged in an affair with the artist Clara Pope.[3] It can be argued, due to the character and religious nature of Curtis, that this is most unlikely to be true.

Curtis has always been described as a happy, cheerful, and amiable family man. This is supported by a character reference written in his obituary: 'Mr Curtis possessed a kind and sympathetic nature which in private life earned for him esteem of many and the love of his children.'[4]

There is a mystery regarding Sarah, namely her relationship to William Curtis. All recorded information about her states that William was her biological father, who was first cousin to Samuel; this means that Samuel had married his second cousin. Jim Gould, writing in the *Garden History Journal* and using information from the Southwark Friends Meeting Minutes Book, disproves to a point that Samuel and Sarah may have been directly related. He states that Sarah was 'a young lady brought up in mysterious circumstances and educated by Samuel's elder cousin, William Curtis.'[5]

Interestingly, around the time of Sarah's birth William had left the Society of Friends (Quakers). It is not known if this was done voluntarily or he was disowned. An argument can be made that Sarah was possibly William's illegitimate daughter or of another close family member. This would explain the connection between her birth and William leaving the Society at that time. Having an illegitimate child would certainly mean being disowned by the Quakers. But a case can be made that she was not William's biological daughter.

Samuel also left the Society of Friends a year after his marriage to Sarah. He was disowned by them for marrying a woman of a different religion. Gould states that:

> 'In 1802 the Friends disowned Samuel, for Sarah was of a different religious persuasion and they had been married "by a Priest contrary to our rules"'.[6]

Curtis was not afraid to voice opinions on matters that he considered important. He did not do this because it would serve for his advancement but because, as a Quaker, it would have been a testimony to the truth, an honest opinion given in good faith and central to Quaker belief. If a truth helped others, for example by increasing productivity or leading to an increase in profits, so providing a better standard of living and improved economic conditions for some, then this would be deemed important and valuable.[7] With this in mind he wrote to the Royal Jersey Agricultural and Horticultural Society (RJA&HS) in 1853 offering his advice based on his experience in farming matters. None of his advice was acted on; undoubtedly some RAJ&HS members would have seen him as an outsider interfering in their business. Curtis was not out to upset people or alienate himself, but simply to tell the truth as he saw it. The following is an extract from the letter:

> 'Gentlemen, I have experienced much pleasure in your delightful Island and favoured climate, and have only a wish to be beneficial to its prosperity in horticulture. I see many parts of the Island capable of growing the products of the South of France. There are many parts capable of growing far more useful things than furze, broom and heath, and I think your attentions would be well directed to the improvement of these wastes.'[8]

Curtis supported the RJA&HS by judging at its flower shows. In 1853 he is listed for the spring, summer and autumn shows as the judge for amateurs and nurserymen's flower and vegetable exhibits. The committee visited La Chaire for a guided tour by Curtis in 1855 and were made very welcome. A report was written on the visit by the society:

> 'We were surprised to see how, in a few years, an unproductive and barren rock had, under the skilful taste and perseverance of that eminent horticulturalist, Samuel Curtis Esq, become a lovely garden, adorned with beautiful specimens of rare and valuable plants, and is now one of the many attractions of the Island.'[9]

Curtis came to Jersey to retire and from 1852 resided permanently at Rozel. However, by 1858 his sight was failing and he became frail. He died at La Chaire in 1860 but the garden planting and maintenance was continued by Harriet, his daughter. La Chaire matured into one of the most remarkable gardens of the Victorian period, a plantsman's garden of note.

After Curtis's death the garden matured fully and became known as La Chaire Tropical Garden, an essential stop on the tourist trail until 1899, when it was closed to the public by Charles Fletcher, the then owner of the property.

Curtis is buried alongside three of his children, the eldest Harriet, Sarah, and his son, William. They lie in St Martin's churchyard, Jersey, approximately two miles from his garden.

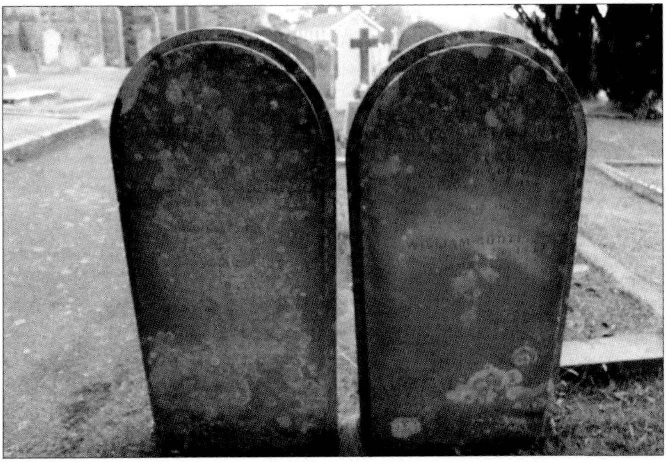

Fig 8 The gravestones for Samuel Curtis, Harriet, Sarah and William

Obituaries appeared in the *Jersey Times*, the *Cottage Gardener* and in the Linnaean Society proceedings. The RJA&HS published their own obituary in 1860:

> 'Samuel Curtis, Esq, of La Chaire. One of the honorary members of the society. Long will he be remembered not only by your committee, but by the strangers and visitors to the Island who invariably received from him a kindly welcome.
>
> The lovely spot where he had fixed his residence showed how the application of scientific observation could convert what seemed a barren hillside into a smiling garden, replete with some very choice specimens of vegetation which are usually to be found only in more Southern climates.

To him the Society is greatly indebted for much valuable information, many important suggestions, a variety of beautifully conducted experiments and the introduction of several new species of plants, fruits and flowers, which had been hitherto uncultivated in the island, whilst his assistance in awarding the premiums at the exhibitions so willingly rendered and so highly prized will be greatly missed for the future.'[10]

In 1788 James Maddock, who was a member of the Society of Friends, sought its permission to marry Mary Curtis, the sister of Samuel. Permission was duly granted as Mary was also a Quaker. James Maddock was the son of James Maddock Senior who founded the floricultural nursery, the Walworth Garden in Southwark, London. The nursery became known as Maddock and Son, and after his father's death James took over the business, producing a vast range of flowers, fruit trees and other plants. In 1792 Maddock produced a 52-page catalogue entitled *A Catalogue of Flowers, Plants and Trees*, sold by Maddock and Son, Florists, at Walworth. A catalogue was produced annually, which included such plants as auricular, polyanthus, carnations, gooseberries, narcissus, tulips, grape vines, peaches and nectarines and many more varied plant types.

In 1798 James, along with his wife, mother and three children moved from the nursery to the seat of the Curtis family at Alton, Hampshire, a change most likely precipitated by financial difficulties. Curtis had stepped in to help save the business of his brother-in-law in 1797. He was supported by Thomas Sturge, another member of the Society of Friends. Sturge was in no way a horticulturist but he was considered a financial genius by Quakers, having saved other businesses owned by members of the Society from bankruptcy. Gould said of Sturge regarding his financial acumen:

> 'He was regarded by Friends as a commercial and financial genius. When only nineteen he had rescued his father from commercial disaster and it was said that relatives could count on his advice and assistance when in difficulty.'[11]

This would support the theory why James Maddock left Walworth and the appearance of Sturge who would not have been involved unless there was a financial crisis. When Curtis married Sarah and was cut off from Friends, which included the support from Sturge, the money that his wife inherited from the death of William Curtis enabled him to carry on running the nursery on his own which undoubtedly saved it from ruin.

Curtis was not a botanist, struggling at times with the correct identification of plants, and while communicating with Hooker at Kew had to describe the plants he wanted as he was unable to name them. This could possibly have been caused naturally by his advancing years. The identification issue can to a small degree be supported by a letter Curtis wrote from La Chaire to Sir William Hooker at Kew, on 1st October, 1853:

> 'I have raised many seedling acacias from the seeds my son sent in letters from the Liverpool plains from the banks of the Namoi River, but as he did not know the names it will be sometime before we know whether they are new or curious.[12]

But to be fair these were new species and were also unknown to his son. Another letter written four years later to Sir William requesting plants, which was sent from La Chaire, dated 30th April 1857, shows more clearly that Curtis had forgotten the names of some species of ferns or that possibly he never knew the names at all: 'Some three years ago you sent me some ferns amongst them were a gold and silver leaved kind but both died after the first winter'[13]

Even though Curtis cannot be considered a botanist he was definitely a plantsman and it can be argued that these plant names should have been familiar. He later grew at La Chaire an extensive range of plants that were classed as exotic, new and rare.

Curtis was primarily a florist (at that time meaning someone who grew flowers at a nursery), the main focus of the business being directed at flower production for the florist trade. In 1792 James Maddock the younger published a book called *The Florist's Directory* that had been penned by his father though not published in his lifetime. The book discussed the cultural requirements of what Maddock considered to be the florist's main flower groups and flowering bulbs, along with a detailed section describing soils and manure. The information provided in this publication was detailed and well written which made the book accessible and proved very popular. Curtis himself produced a second edition in 1810 using it to promote the Walworth nursery that he was now managing, and to push specific plants that were being produced for sale. He also extended the cultural information included in the first addition. Curtis published a third expanded and final *Florist's Directory* in 1822, increasing the plant range included in the previous editions. In the final publication he included information on the dahlia, chrysanthemum, lobelia and the mignonette tree. The mignonette is the common name (as well as Egyptian privet), for *Lawsonia inermis* – henna. The inclusion of henna shows that Curtis was keen to cultivate plants that were considered unusual, something he strived to achieve later at La Chaire in the range of rare and exotic plants he grew there.

While he was at Walworth, Curtis found time to publish a series of botanical lectures that had been given by his late cousin, William. The transcripts were a collection of the lectures William had given in London and entitled: *Lectures on botany, as delivered in the Botanic garden at Lambeth*. They extended to three volumes and included in the third volume a brief biography of William's life.

In 1806 Samuel Curtis commenced publishing a work in his own name, entitled *The Beauties of Flora*. The coloured engravings, large in size, being 28 x 24 inches were produced by Thomas Baxter and Clara Marie Pope, both prominent artists and illustrators at the time. Each engraving demonstrates a range of varieties from one of the eight established floristry plant groups at that time, the first displaying tulip and ranunculus. There were also two engravings devoted entirely to dahlias. All the engravings were of the highest quality and used as the subject material for plants cultivated at Walworth. There was an explanatory text in French and English. The work culminated in 1820 with a volume that contained all ten engravings with a retail value of £5.

The management of the Walworth nursery, as well as the lectures that he published, his input into *The Florist's Directory* and his work on *Beauties of Flora* were vital tools in Curtis gaining experience in not only horticulture but in writing and publishing. The Walworth nursery was an important step in his acquiring knowledge and experience in horticultural techniques. He became skilful in the care and cultivation of fruit and ornamental trees and shrubs. After 1815 information on the nursery becomes unclear; it no longer featured in the London directories and records of it are not available for the period up to the 1830s. But then it reappeared in records, showing that it had a new owner up until 1843.[14]

In 1827, after the death of his wife who had inherited the publication *The Botanical Magazine* from William Curtis, Samuel took over as sole proprietor. By then the magazine had been in publication for 30 years. Sarah's death, on 2nd July 1827, left him to bring up their 13 children, the youngest of whom was Georgina, then three-years old. The *Curtis Botanical Magazine*, as he retitled it, became the precursor for the majority of modern-day horticultural publications and still technically in print under the name *The Garden*, the magazine of the Royal Horticultural Society. During 1827 William Jackson Hooker was made editor. This formed the start of a longstanding friendship between the two men, although at times it became severely strained, Hooker becoming frustrated over late and irregular salary payments. He communicated this by letter:

> 'Curtis is not a fit publisher for the magazine. Every letter I have is full of complaints of the sales being worse and worse: so that unless it gets into better hands I cannot conceive that it can continue to yield a return for the expenses upon it. An opinion prevails that I do not make the magazine sufficiently popular.[15]

The rift in their friendship did not last long. Later Hooker supported Curtis with his acquisition of plants for La Chaire and recommended him for the laying out of Victoria Park, Bethnal Green, which was completed in 1845. High praise was accorded to Curtis by Hooker to the park commissioners which ensured Curtis acquired the commission. A. B. Burleigh wrote: 'The highest testimony was borne by Sir William Hooker, Director of the Royal Botanical Garden at Kew.'[16] Curtis himself selected all the trees and shrubs for the park. The success of this commission led to him being appointed to design the Nottingham Arboretum which was opened in 1852.

In 1805 Curtis decided that the Walworth nursery was not suitable for his plans to grow the type of plants he really wished to cultivate, so he searched for a suitable property and found Glazenwood in Essex. Curtis writing in the third person explains the reason for this move:

> 'About the year 1805, Mr Curtis, to his extensive cultivation of flowers, as a florist, at Walworth, near London, was desirous to unite a perfect knowledge of every kind of useful and ornamental gardening than had hitherto been practised in England. With this view he anxiously sought for a spot of land for that purpose, and Glazenwood opportunely offering itself to his notice, he purchased it, and immediately adopted his favourite object of collecting, from every part...the finest kinds of apples and other hardy fruit trees.'[17]

Curtis bought Glazenwood in 1805 but did not live there permanently until 1808. The sequence of events regarding owning and living at Walworth and Glazenwood are hazy but Curtis found and purchased a house on the Glazenwood estate in 1805. He continued to own the Walworth nursery but moved to Glazenwood in 1808. After working for the Duke of Newcastle at Clumber, Nottinghamshire, and residing there from 1816 to 1821, he moved back to Glazenwood. During his employment by the Duke, Curtis had bought the entire Glazenwood estate from Joseph Greenwood and increased the number of buildings.

In 1808, while at Glazenwood, Curtis was awarded a silver medal from the Society of Arts for planting an extensive orchard. Curtis informed them of his undertakings by letter. The citation from the Society was full of praise and read: 'His exertions in having planted the most extensive orchard in the kingdom and, also, for his communications to the Society on horticultural matters.'[18]

On 20th November, 1810, Curtis was made a fellow of the Linnaean Society. In this year he also published a rare and still sought after book, *The Finest Flowering Shrubs and Curious Plants*. It can be argued that this work fuelled his desire to grow rare and unusual plants at Glazenwood, and later at La Chaire.

While retaining ownership of Glazenwood, Curtis was employed by the Duke of Newcastle at Clumber. He was employed as his Land Agent and lived at Gamston Hall. Curtis was responsible for paying a sum of £4,000 per year in wages to the Duke's employees. While living at Gamston Hall, Curtis produced the now famous work, *Monograph on the Genus Camellia*, which documented the hybridising that had taken place in the late eighteenth century with *Camellia japonica*. He completed this in 1819, with illustrations of eleven varieties of Camellia that had been introduced from the Orient. The artist he commissioned was Clara Marie Pope who was already well known to him. The work was dedicated to his employer's wife, Her Grace Georgiana Elizabeth, Duchess of Newcastle. In 1821 Curtis completed his work for the Duke and moved back to Glazenwood. He then set about building a villa near the original house and erecting glasshouses.

Even while residing at Gamston Hall, Curtis was building a solid horticultural reputation at Glazenwood. He was said to grow

> 'Every kind of tree of note known to exist in the British Isles. Amongst these were the rare *Ginkgo biloba*, the Maidenhair tree, and *Quercus phellos*, the Willow oak, from N. America.'[19]

By the late 1820s Curtis had turned Glazenwood into a garden of considerable note which was in part inspired by the Royal Botanical Gardens at Kew.

In 1831 Curtis began experimenting with growing tender exotic plants at Glazenwood, something that was to become the core of his later work at La Chaire. Curtis also described what was being achieved with his orchards. In a pamphlet he wrote about his collection of 7,000 apple trees, 3,000 pears, 1,500 cherries and other top fruit. This pamphlet was designed to attract subscriptions from potential visiting subscribers to Glazenwood. For their subscription they could receive free fruit and visit the garden whenever they wished to do so:

> 'Mr Curtis left Walworth to reside at, and to cultivate this chosen spot… until it became the favourite resort of many distinguished cultivators; and the specimens of American shrubs usually considered capable of thriving only in peat, or heath-mould, are seen growing to gigantic sizes in loam.'[20]

In 1831 Curtis gives an insight into the planting at Glazenwood and the best idea of what was to later follow at La Chaire:

> 'Of the more tender exotic plants in this collection, there are a great variety of the most ornamental kinds, kept in greenhouses, and numerous pits and frames; besides, upwards of six hundred of the finest kinds of Roses; an excellent collection of dahlias, &c. The whole is surrounded by agreeable walks, and suitable accommodation is afforded to visitors for taking such refreshments as they may bring for themselves.'[21]

Proof that Curtis was experimenting with growing rare and exotic plants from America and Australia can be found in the details of a garden party held at Glazenwood.[22] The article names plants that were later to feature at La Chaire, such as *Wisteria consequana*, double blossom pomegranate, and magnolia. The garden had a grove named Australia which was full of rare, half-hardy and non-hardy plants. Limited success cultivating these plants at Glazenwood was instrumental in Curtis looking for a new site in Great Britain where they could be grown in comparative safety from severe weather. Essex does have the advantage of the lowest rainfall in the United Kingdom and a free draining soil overall, but frosts and snow are common. During the winters of 1837-8 Curtis experienced many losses due to the weather, mainly in his beloved Australasian species.

Curtis realised that he could not push back the botanical boundaries in Essex, the climate and topography were against him. He eventually found what he considered to be the perfect position for a garden, on the island of Jersey.

~ 2 ~

Samuel Curtis comes to Jersey

Curtis started looking for a situation in England that would not restrict the rare, non-hardy, and half-hardy exotic plants he wished to cultivate. Samuel's search led him to Jersey, where in a verdant valley next to the sea at Rozel, the climate and geology matched his criteria. Tony Russell, the short-term horticultural director of La Chaire in 2003/4, wrote:

> 'He then began a search to find a suitable location for growing subtropical plants from the Mediterranean, Australasia and South Africa. This search took him from the west coast of Scotland to Cornwall. His objectives were clear – he wanted to establish the biggest collection of subtropical plants ever grown outside in the British Isles. In the spring of 1841 he found the sheltered Rozel valley on the east coast of Jersey. Within weeks, Curtis had purchased 10ha (24 acres) of the valley and began to build a house for himself and his daughter Harriet.'[23]

It is worth noting here that people familiar with Jersey state that the west coast rather than the east coast has a far better climate suited to tropical plants. This is illustrated by a house named Belle Vue in St Aubin, on the west side of the Island. It has had tropical plants growing in its garden for well over 150 years that have escaped the frosts and snow which have at times decimated the garden at La Chaire on the east side. But Curtis did not consider the geology acceptable in the west. Much later Charles Fletcher, during his tenure of La Chaire, overcame this problem by creating deep planting pockets, bringing in hundreds of tons of soil. Curtis perhaps lacked the funds to do this and was probably daunted by the sheer logistical problems in moving soil up to the top of the garden, a height of around 300 feet. Fletcher had a machine constructed, moving trolleys on winches and cables to move his soil.

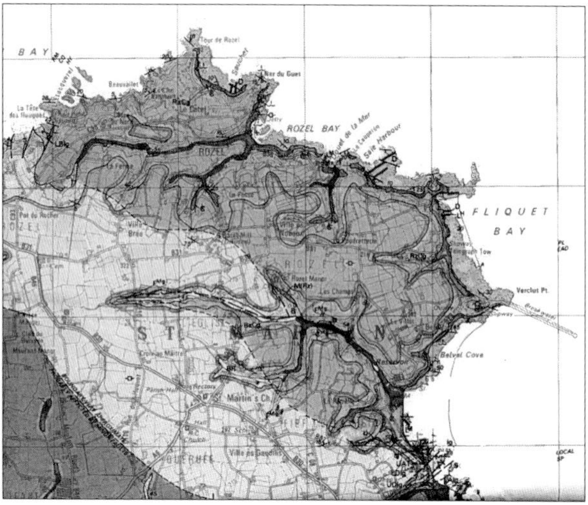

Fig 9 The darker shaded central area shows the position of Rozel Conglomerate or puddingstone.[24] ©British Geological Survey

There was one important factor at La Chaire that made it suitable for tropical plants. This was the local bedrock known as Rozel conglomerate. It is a purple puddingstone and is only found in the north-east of Jersey.[25] The rest of the island is composed mainly of impenetrable granite. Rozel conglomerate is a sedimentary rock that in this area occurs near or at the surface of the land. The rock has been weathered chemically, by freeze/thaw action, oxidation and hydrolysis. The area was also covered by deposits of windblown (loess) clay and silt that arrived from the Continent during the Pleistocene Ice Ages. This varies in depth from 1 to 3 metres, whch has been subject to erosion, and there is a mix of soil and humic levels most likely due to bioturbation.

Curtis saw the mix of mudstones, siltstones and red sandstones holding predominately rounded, slightly irregular clasts of stone, which consist of shale, andesite, rhyolite (volcanic) and ignimbrite, making this a polymict-clast type formation. The importance of this rock to Curtis was that it is easily broken up and can be penetrated by plant roots. The clasts improve drainage and render the soil free draining which is perfect for tropical plants. The pH is lower than seven making it acidic, supporting the plant types that were chosen, especially the rhododendrons on the northern section of the valley garden. Curtis had found the correct bedrock and soil type. He now just needed a suitable climate.

The north-east of Jersey has a much gentler coastline, contrasting with the high sheer cliffs further along the north coast. But it is these northern cliffs and headlands that protect Rozel from the prevailing winds. The Rozel area is characterised by wooded valleys. La Chaire is in the Rozel Valley and although the garden reaches a height of over 300 feet it is well defended from the elements. This is reflected in the most even, undamaged tree growth on the island.

This natural defence would have been a key factor for Curtis. What may not have been a key factor in the search for the perfect location is that this part of the coast affords breathtaking views of the offshore reef known as Les Ecrehous and the Normandy coast.[26] Normandy on the French mainland is only 15 miles distant.

Curtis would have studied the temperature charts for Jersey and was almost correct in deciding that La Chaire was a frost-free location.[27] This was a fair assumption, as La Chaire lay protected in a steep valley just 100 metres from the sea. The warm sea keeps the temperature far higher than mainland France or England. The sea's effect is lessened at the centre of the Island which is significantly cooler than the coast. But La Chaire would not have been immune from severe weather, especially low temperatures that move in on the east to south-east winds. Curtis compensated for this by planting a heavy *Quercus ilex* windbreak to the east, and also as extra protection to the west. Despite all his investigations he was sadly disillusioned by the winter weather in 1842. Extremely cold air moved in from the east and created havoc in the garden. Writing to his son James, Curtis describes this:

> 'I had supposed from all I heard that a Jersey winter was a very harmless one, and so mild as to let us enjoy out of doors with but little interruption, however, it is I daresay worse than any person on the Island ever before

> remembers it. Last Friday, Saturday and Sunday, we had a frosty easterly wind, attended with a scotch mist and drizzling rain. As fast as it fell it froze on to everything it touched and the accumulation of the 3 days coated every twig with ice as transparent as glass, so that the slender twigs of a tamarisk opposite to our window were encrusted with ice an inch and a half in diameter, and all the trees were so loaded in the same manner that the weight of ice began to break and spilt the boughs down, and had a brisk wind sprung up every tree must have been ruined. On Monday morning it began to thaw, it was still foggy and we walked out to see the mischief which was done and still going on. There was previously about 4 inches of snow on the ground, which was coated with ice so as to be as sonorous as a drum; in our walk we could hear branches fall ¼ of a mile from us, and so perpetual was the crashes in all directions about us, that it was like listening to the distant discharge of musketry.'[28]

The most devastating year for La Chaire came long after Curtis had died. The Great Blizzard in 1895 destroyed most of the trees, shrubs and plants that Curtis had collected and planted.

Recorded climate information is patchy but weather records show that in 1854 the average temperature was 4.4°C in January and 5.0°C in February, falling to -2.8°C for one day in February, not enough to cause major problems but a sharp enough dip to kill plants. Worse came in 1855: in January there was a cold snap, the temperature falling to -5.6°C from an average that month of 3.6°C. February of 1855 shows a very low mean temperature of 0.6°C. The February mean for the turn of the nineteenth century was 5.9C. On average, winter temperatures in Jersey do not fall below freezing, although if this does happen it is usually for short periods of time. Sometimes the dip can be significant and is enough to cause damage. In 1856 the average winter temperature was 9.4°C but for one day in January it fell to -3.9°C. This non-stable pattern does not support non-hardy plants that are susceptible to sudden fluctuations.

So La Chaire was not the haven for tropical plants that Curtis thought it would be. The point can be argued that he was misguided with plants being destroyed in 1841, again in 1855 and then all but wiped out in 1895. The mean temperature during the winter months is by comparison to the mainland far higher, but Jersey is vulnerable to these sudden temperature reversals that can cause major problems. The situation of La Chaire in terms of the geology was excellent, but unfortunately it was not the perfect location for climate. Curtis believed La Chaire was a frost-free location but this was not the case.

~ 3 ~

Victorian gardens in England and Jersey

The garden of La Chaire was constructed primarily to harvest the rich and diverse range of plants that were entering Great Britain through establishments such as the Kew Botanical Garden and the Veitch Nursery. Private plant hunters were sponsored by botanical gardens, nurseries, and individual collectors to bring back new, rare and exotic wonders.

Many factors led to the procurement and subsequent arrival of new plant species during the nineteenth century. China was encouraged to open its borders and to trade with Europe and America. There were increased, faster, and more efficient methods of transport, shortening the time to travel long distances and ensuring plants arrived in better condition. This was aided by the support of inventions such as the Wardian case, which revolutionised plant transportation. The proliferation of horticultural publications in the nineteenth century helped to shape fashion and create a demand for new plants. The emergence of horticultural periodicals and catalogues and their overall effect cannot be overstated, as they showcased new plant arrivals and included cultural information. This increased awareness of what was, and what could potentially become available. They also provided information on plant care. One such example was the publication named *Botanical Cabinet*, described by Hobhouse:

> 'In 1815, the celebrated nursery firm of Loddiges in Hackney established the Botanical Cabinet as a monthly illustrated periodical and catalogue to its vast collection of plants.'[29]

This magazine had a wide readership secured through the continual development of printing and the reproduction of colour illustrations in an inexpensive format. The *Botanical Cabinet* displayed a wealth of new plant material. The oldest of the magazines was *The Botanical Magazine* founded by William Curtis. John Claudius Loudon was another publisher, journalist and author. He produced *The Gardeners Magazine* in 1826 having already written *The Encyclopaedia of Gardening* in 1822. Because of Loudon's influence, the 'Picturesque Garden' as advocated by Price and Gilpin underwent a change, it transformed into a new style known as the 'Gardenesque'. The rough, rugged and irregular Picturesque landscape began to change. Picturesque woodlands and valleys were converted into sites in which to display Himalayan plants and exotics from America as described here by Turner:

> 'In the second half of the nineteenth century many woodland valleys were converted into 'natural compositions' of exotics. Himalayan plants (e.g. rhododendrons and camellias) and North American plants proved particularly well suited to this idea.'[30]

Loudon suggested that plants be displayed so they looked pleasing from all angles, hence his preference for round beds. He also believed that a garden must include non-native species, and that this should be the garden's primary role. The Gardenesque style became the setting to showcase new plant arrivals. Loudon went on to say the Gardenesque was:

> 'more suitable for those persons who are botanists, rather than general admirers of scenery, because it is best calculated for displaying the individual beauty of trees and plants.'[31]

Defining a Victorian garden with any real clarity is problematic. They often resulted in a collection of motifs, a pastiche of many different historical styles with elements of Dutch, Italian, and French baroque, mixed with carpets of mass bedding in ornate parterres which were designed and carried through by men such as William Nesfield. It is important to note that the formal style was continued during the Victorian era. The rich still displayed their wealth and social standing through a formal garden as explained by this statement:

> 'It was not surprising that, coexisting with the development of the Gardenesque, there was a movement back to designs dominated by architecture in the more imposing landscapes. In an age of wealth and expansionism, structured terraces, steps and fountains made the perfect setting to showcase not only the lifestyles of rich owners but also the myriad plants unavailable to previous generations.'[32]

There was a frenetic zeal in creating the most eclectic gardens. The following passage supports the idea of Victorian eclecticism in garden design and a lack of definition:

> 'It is impossible to define a typical Victorian garden. it was often a pastiche of the picturesque and the geometrical, of exotic and indigenous trees, of standard roses rising above drifts of old-fashioned flowers or in regimented beds, of serpentine walks and shrubberies, of stretches of lawn with a Wellingtonia or a monkey puzzle tree standing guard, and with a rustic seat or arbour from which to contemplate it all.'[33]

The only constant in the ever-changing horticultural world was the use of newly collected plants and Samuel Curtis was at the forefront of this.

The inference that La Chaire was designed by Curtis in the Gardenesque style cannot be conclusively proved as he left no documentation to support this. But consequently none exists to support that it was not. Curtis did use plants in a more relaxed way than true Gardenesque, but there was still a series of similarities between the Gardensque style and the garden at La Chaire. There was undoubtedly a linking philosophy between Loudon and Curtis. Arguably the topography of the steep valley at Rozel did not make Loudon's principle of seeing plants as individuals completely possible, and space was also at a premium. But Curtis did use new and exotic plants and his aim was that some of the plants he cultivated could and should be grown to improve knowledge and understanding, thus benefiting the economic status of the landowner.

Curtis experimented with growing tea at La Chaire and aimed to become self-sufficient with this crop. La Chaire was an experimental garden. Producing tea would show farmers that they could grow it, so providing increased income for Jersey and local people. Loudon also held thoughts on this philosophy and said that such places would help working men to educate themselves and thus improve their economic status.

Both Curtis and Loudon used plants in settings that evoked their natural location, such as with the rhododendrons that Curtis planted on the north side of the natural valley in his Himalayan glade. La Chaire was first and foremost designed as a plantsman's garden and not a garden designed in the Picturesque style converted to the Gardenesque, even though the topography would have made without doubt one of the most exciting and challenging Picturesque landscapes.

Again there is no documentation to support the suggestion that Curtis was influenced by Loudon, but it is inconceivable that Curtis as a publisher and writer did not at least look at work written by this highly respected and influential man. It is unlikely that Curtis did not aspire to some of Loudon's ideas and philosophy. Both men strove to improve the horticultural techniques of landowners and employees as well as their skills and knowledge. They both saw education as the way forward. Curtis aimed to increase agricultural techniques and so profitability, as already discussed.[34] He used the philosophy of Quaker honesty, suggesting ideas based on experience that, if successful, would result in increased productivity and profit for all, this eventually being passed down the line so society as a whole would benefit. Loudon used the written word and argument to educate, as stated here:

> 'Loudon's constant aim was to better the human condition through greater knowledge, and he published some 66 million words to that end. Ever higher-minded, with a streak of Calvinistic zeal, he sought to educate both employers and their gardeners, and to find ways of improving the working conditions of the latter.[35]

Both men had such similar ideas and must have known each other through membership of the Linnaean Society. Loudon became a member in 1806 and

Curtis in 1810. Both experimented in growing new and exotic plants and both laid out a new arboretum. In 1839 Loudon designed the Derby arboretum and Curtis the Nottingham arboretum in 1852. Without doubt Loudon would have approved of what Curtis achieved at La Chaire, a plantsman's garden with elements of the Gardenesque. He would also have approved of Curtis's Quaker truthfulness and honesty with its aim of unselfish improvement.

Curtis did not have the only garden of horticultural merit in Jersey. Sir John Le Couteur owned Belle Vue in the parish of St Brelade and had a well-stocked garden. Both gardens housed a collection of rare and exotic plants. Sir John enjoyed everything horticultural, visiting as many gardens as possible and being a regular exhibitor at local flower shows where he often won prizes for his flowers, fruit and vegetables. There were large quantities of fruit grown at Belle Vue, even exotic types such as oranges. In 1834 a basket of pears, the variety 'Belle de Jersey' was sent as a gift to William IV who enjoyed them very much. Then in 1841the best examples of the pear, *'La Duchesse d' Angoulême'* were sent to Queen Victoria and placed on her table.

Curtis and Sir John became very good friends, each visiting the other's garden on more than one occasion. Curtis said of Belle Vue that he was, 'Surprised at the number of rare plants growing at Belle Vue, the prettiest spot in the Island.'[36] Curtis would have appreciated Sir John's plant choice as he was dedicated to growing rare plants himself at La Chaire. Sir John would take visitors to see Curtis's garden and he very much admired it. He wrote about La Chaire in his diary and called it:

> 'Italy in Jersey and a pretty rock garden. The occupants are Mr Curtis the author of the *Botanical Magazine*, and Mrs Fothergill his daughter. Harriet and I drove to La Chaire to lunch with Mr Curtis and Mrs Fothergill. We were there until 5 looking at his lovely and rare plants, several of which he gave us. One day he loaded our gig with pretty plants for the wilderness. A fine old patriarch of 83. Gave my wife his blessing and good wishes for the New Year, and a kiss.'[37]

Like Curtis, Sir John also received plants from Kew. Some of Sir John's plants were early introductions and included: *Magnolia obovata, Magnolia auriculata* (introduced from America in 1786), *Magnolia fuscata* (introduced from China in 1789) and *Berberis coriacea* (introduced from Nepal in 1818). Belle Vue and La Chaire would appear to be very alike with plants arriving via Kew from America, China, Nepal, India and Australia. Joan Stevens explains the provenance of some of the Belle Vue planting:

> 'There is a list of 73 types of geranium. A consignment of roses from a nurseryman in Caen included 60 varieties, none of which is well known now, such as Prince Albert, the Duchess of Kent and Elizabeth Fry. Seeds were received from India, Australia and the penal settlement, Norfolk Island, and raised with care at Belle Vue.'[38]

In the nineteenth century Jersey had many nurseries, some of these being included on the tourist trail with excursion cars paying weekly visits. There were many other Island attractions including La Chaire that also received visitors.

The Nursery firm Langellier of St Helier held over 30,000 Camellia stocks in 1850, while Saunders who supplied trees were important enough to receive a visit from Queen Victoria during her royal visit in 1846. Sir John and Curtis may have been provided with plants by both these nurseries, considering in particular that they sold camellias and trees.

~ 4 ~

Plant types Samuel Curtis used at La Chaire

Curtis had a desire to grow half-hardy and non-hardy plants of all species. This included plants that might have economic possibilities, so benefiting local growers. First and foremost Curtis considered himself an experimental gardener, in a letter to his family he wrote during 1854 from La Chaire he displays this philosophy:

We have thousands of chrysanthemums still in blossom of which we prefer the small pompom varieties.

I have lately turned my attention to half hardy shrubs and plants such as require protection in England. Marie is to bring me more plants from Kew and the Botanic Garden in Regents Park. They keep me well supplied with curious plants and I am trying to make some new rock work and want all the best plants for it, but at present until it is planted it looks like Sebastopol! I have more than thirty tall stems of Yucca gloriosa in blossom at once.[39]

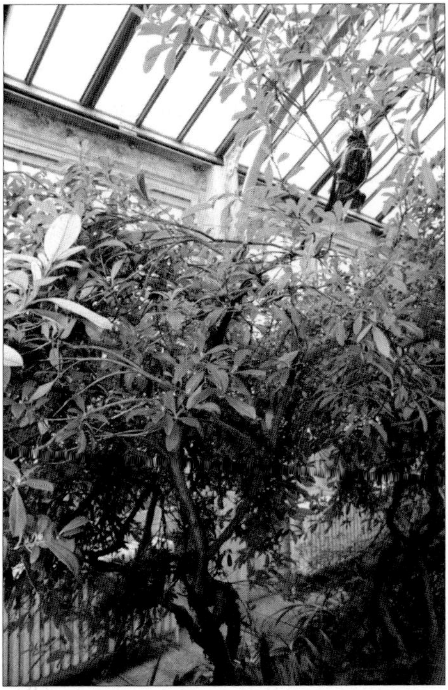

Fig 10 *Rhododendron ciliatum* a non-hardy Rhododendron grown outside at La Chaire in the Himalayan glade, on the north side of the garden. This plant will not tolerate prolonged temperatures below 5°F.

An example of the experiments Curtis embarked upon in growing rare plants can be recognised today at The Royal Botanic Gardens, Kew. Curtis requested from Kew, *Rhododendron ciliatum*, which in England can be grown only when shielded from the autumn and winter weather. This rhododendron was discovered by Joseph Dalton Hooker while on a plant-hunting expedition in Sikkim between 1848 and 1850. Curtis grew it successfully in the Himalayan glade on the north side of the garden, while at Kew it has to be grown under glass.

Another non-hardy rhododendron grown at La Chaire was *Rhododendron dalhousiae*. This plant will not tolerate anything but mild temperatures. The flower buds of this plant are even more intolerant to low temperatures.

Growing these susceptible plants was obviously a risk.

The plant hunting expedition that Joseph D. Hooker undertook to collect these rhododendrons heralded a period of great plant discovery, signifying the start of the Sino-Himalayan rhododendron collections. Curtis was receiving these plants just a short time after their introduction into the UK, putting La Chaire (and Kew) at the forefront of growing new, rare and important plants.

The north facing side of the valley garden afforded protection to the non-hardy rhododendrons. *Quercus ilex* and *Ulmus x sarniensis* were already growing naturally on this gentler sloping side, protecting plants beneath them and creating a micro climate. *Quercus ilex* is at its extreme northern range in Jersey and is classed as indigenous. It grew in what became Jersey before the English Channel removed the land bridge between it and mainland France. Tony Russell has written that:

> The north-facing valley side was not quite so steep and covered with lush vegetation comprising evergreen oak, Quercus ilex and Jersey elm, Ulmus x sarniensis. It had the warmth of the Mediterranean coupled with the humidity of Chile or Tasmania.[40]

Quercus ilex played a vital role in the garden as Curtis planted it in depth all along the Western, northern and eastern edges of the garden. He planted these deep shelterbelts to provide protection for his tender plants.

Rhododendrons were majorly represented in the Himalayan garden. Curtis planted groups of *Rhododendron arboreum, R. falconeri, R. campanulatum, R. edgeworthii*, and a hybrid that had been bred by Curtis at La Chaire between *R. formosum* and *R. edgeworthii*, making *R. formosum x edgeworthii.* Curtis when writing to Sir William Hooker at Kew requested plants he wished to grow. These requests included a large selection of rhododendrons. There were rhododendrons recorded growing at La Chaire that had been recorded growing at Glazenwood.[41]

A plant that can only be grown in a large heated conservatory is *Strelitzia reginae*. It is non-hardy planted outside in northern Europe, and can only be grown unprotected in places such as southern Spain, but Curtis grew this plant successfully at La Chaire. *Strelitzia* was introduced to Kew from South

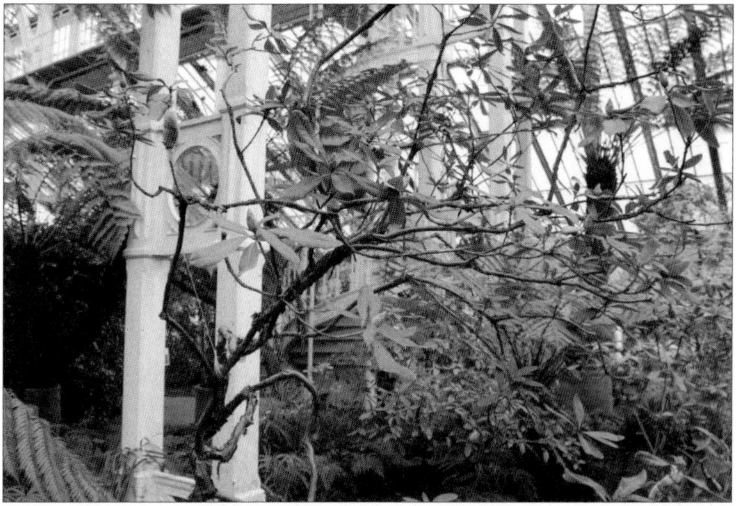

Fig 11 *Rhododendron dalhousiae* was discovered in 1849 and grown outside at La Chaire. Joseph D. Hooker called it 'the noblest species of the whole race'". This example is grown under glass at Kew.

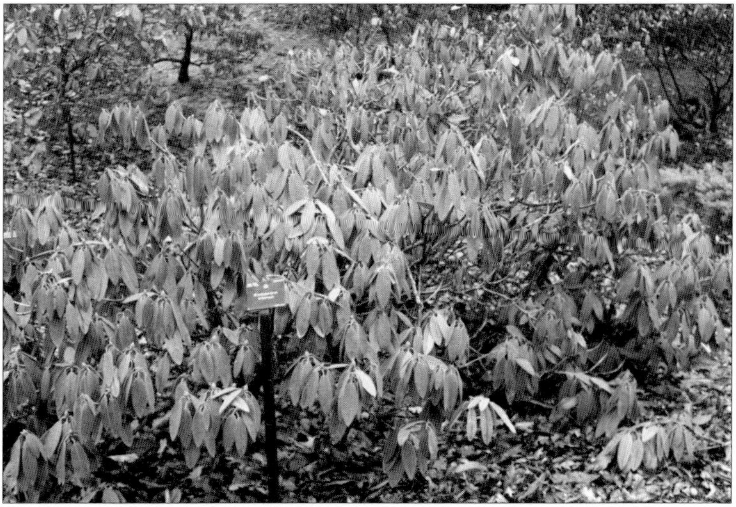

Fig 12 *Rhododendron arboreum* which is still found at Kew. It was planted by Curtis at La Chaire in the Himalayan glade.

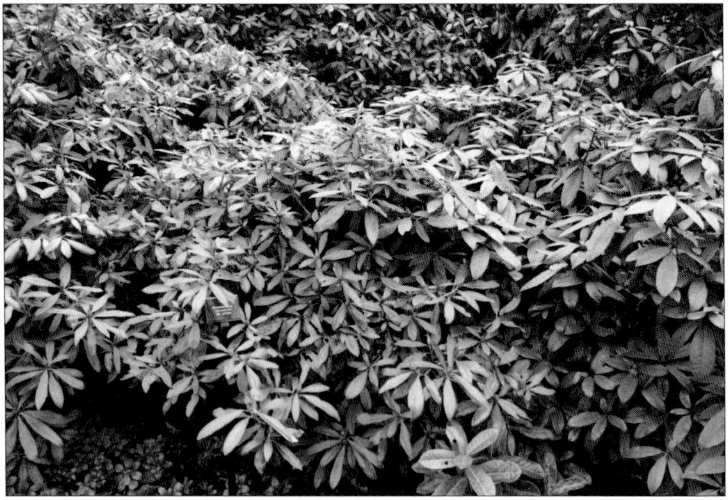

Fig 13 *Rhododendron caucasicum* which was grown at Glazenwood by Curtis, and also recorded as being planted at La Chaire. This rhododendron is hardy, unlike most of the others that Curtis planted at La Chaire.

Africa in 1773 by their first plant hunter, Francis Masson. During the proposed restoration period at La Chaire, the BBC along with Chris Beardshaw produced a 30-minute documentary entitled *More Hidden Gardens*. The program aired in 2004, and for the cameras Beardshaw and Russell planted around six *Strelitzia reginea* near the summit of the garden at the eastern corner. The idea being that these plants were the first ones to be replanted for the restoration project. The restoration failed and the *Strelitzia* were forgotten, but they have survived the Jersey climate and are still growing today. They are not big and have obviously not thrived. But despite having received nothing in the way of maintenance or protection for the last nine years they are still alive. If any plant can be indicative of what Curtis was striving to achieve then *Strelitzia* is that plant.

When in June 1855 members of the Royal Jersey Agricultural and Horticultural Society were given a tour of La Chaire and wrote their report on the visit, they discussed the uniqueness of the garden Curtis had created and the non-hardy exotics he grew:

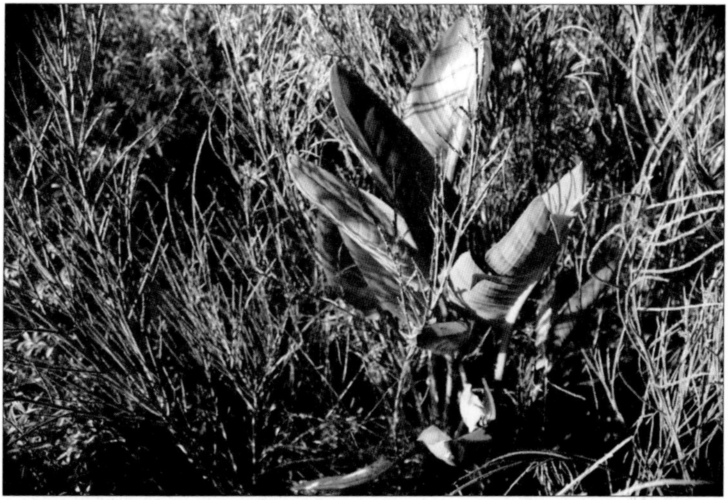

Fig 14 One of the *Strelitzia reginea* planted in 2004 at la Chaire for the TV program *More Hidden Gardens*. This plant is a testament to Curtis and what he was trying to achieve at La Chaire in growing new, rare, and exotic plants.

'The ground has been cleared and levelled and a neat residence erected thereon. Behind and on every side it is surrounded with terraces most romantically situated among the rocks bearing flowers, fruit and vegetables of great variety and in the highest perfection. Numerous rare exotics heretofore in England to be found only under glass carefully tended are at La Chaire by skilful management and judgment in a choice of situation produced luxuriously in the open air. The spot seems a species of fairy land.'[42]

This uniqueness manifested itself in other plant choices that were unusual, but again demonstrated a fundamental wish to improve the Jersey economy if successful. Curtis planted *Thea viridis* to experiment with the possibilities of growing tea as a crop in Jersey.[43] He also grew sugar cane and yams, or as he referred to them, Chinese potatoes. Curtis wrote about these plants in a letter dated October 1854:

Tell everyone that my sugar cane, sown in April is eight feet tall, so dense a mass that a cat could not get amongst it. My Yams or Chinese potatoes look well. I have about 120 pots planted and to plant out, so next winter I hope, if I live so long, to prove their worth.[44]

He also enjoyed producing fruit and makes reference to making his own jam made from fruit grown at La Chaire: 'Today we made 12 bottles of jam from our own Madeira whortleberries, I think it excellent. No one else has it.'[45]

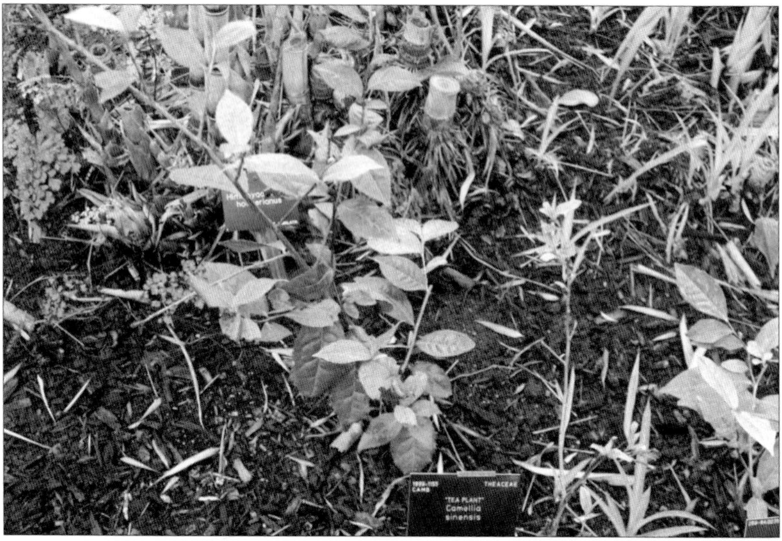

Fig 15 *Camellia sinensis* can be found growing at Kew. Curtis experimented with producing tea as a new potential crop for Jersey and as a way of improving the economy.

La Chaire was a riot of colour and packed with plants from many parts of the world. Russell gives some idea of how the garden would have looked:

'Dozens of acacias, *Eriobotrya japonica, Thea viridis* and members of the Olive family, Olea sativa and fragrans. Along paths winding up from the house were masses of South African, *Mesembryanthemum tricolor*, very much at home amongst the steep, sunny rocky crevices.'[46]

Other accounts exist of how La Chaire appeared, all describing in wonder the overwhelming variety of plant species that were cultivated. In 1858 Curtis welcomed Adam White, a visitor from the Linnaean Society, to La Chaire. White wrote a detailed account of what he discovered:

> 'Curtis was struck with the sheltered situation of the bay, and thought of it as a place to which he would like to retire. For a trifling sum he purchased the rock and immediately began to transform it into a Chinese garden. It was so steep and bare, that, excepting a scanty sprinkling of rock flowers, it produced nothing and seemed incapable of being turned to any account. By quarrying the rock, however, he made a smooth surface on which he built a house, and by dint of labour he carried winding walks to the top, and succeeded in bringing up some of the rich vegetable soil of the island, with which he filled artificial fissures and hollows in the rock. The result was, that in a few years La Chaire was covered with a mass of the most varied vegetation, and in 1858 Mr Curtis informed Mr White that he had at least 2,000 different species of plants, shrubs, trees, and flowers, growing in the utmost luxurance on what a few years before was a bare rock. Shrubs that require a greenhouse even in the Isle of Wight, stood all seasons at Rozel Bay without any injury.'[47]

A further picture of the garden can be gleaned from a letter sent to Sir William Hooker from La Chaire on 30th April, 1857. The letter demonstrates that communication to Kew was taking place and that Curtis was asking for plants, and was propagating them if possible to do so. He was also asking for half-hardy species. Again the letter shows that La Chaire was at the forefront of new introductions, as the plant which was written about was *Eugenia ugni*. This had only been introduced into England by William Lobb in 1844. Curtis enjoyed the unusual and this plant with its spice-scented leaves and cranberry-like fruits fitted his criteria. The *Eugenia ugni*, or amongst many other common names, the New Zealand Cranberry, was reported to be the favourite fruit of Queen Victoria.[48] It does not tolerate cold winters so could be grown comparatively safely in Cornwall. Here nurseries aimed to grow it commercially for fruit production, using in their marketing material the knowledge that it was the Queen's favoured fruit. Curtis had obviously and previously asked about its ease of propagation, so it is quite possible he was considering experimenting with growing it as another potentially economically enhancing crop for Jersey's nurseries and farms. The quote below is a fairly straightforward request for plant material but typifies everything that Curtis was trying to achieve at La Chaire. If Curtis had come to Jersey earlier in his life, farming and nursery production could very well have been vastly different following the first decades after his death. He wrote:

> I have a good account of the *Eugenia ugni*. I hear you speak of it as easy of propagation therefore if Mr Smith could spare me some of it I will try to grow it in our mild climate, if I had some cuttings Mr Smith would know whether I could strike them. I am fond of trying the half hardy.[49]

He also asked Sir William for plants simply based on their aesthetic value with no other motive than to enhance the beauty of the garden. Curtis requested that Sir William send him Rosa Fortunes Double Yellow, also known as Beauty of Glazenwood, as it would complement his Rosa Cloth of Gold. Curtis wrote that his Cloth of Gold had blooms 40 feet apart. He also asked for wisteria, *Fothergilla gardenia* and *Fothergilla major*.[50] Evidence again that pure aesthetics were important can be found in a letter written to Sir William on 1st October, 1853. Curtis was requesting that Himalayan plants be sent to him but that he would prefer the more ornamental type over rare or simply functional.[51]

Curtis obviously loved La Chaire and from his letters the garden seemed to be a mass of colour. He enjoyed showing people around even in old age when he became frail. In one letter to Sir William he tells him how he feels about the garden and that it is: Our paradise regained, a happy valley.[52]

He goes onto describe to Sir William how the garden was looking, 'At the present time I could show you much rhododendron, epacris, mesembryanthumum, Erica and roses in fine bloom.'[53]

Not every plant was a success. He wrote about an acacia that he thought was *Acacia umbrosa* but which turned out to be anything but. It was felled for timber. An illustration of *Acacia umbrosa* had appeared in the *Botanical Magazine* during 1843, painted from an original drawing by Sir William Hooker, so identification should not have been too difficult. He had more success with *Acacia sophorae*, a striking tree from south-eastern Australia with bright yellow flowers, he wrote, '*Acacia sophorae* is beautiful full of golden blooms 15ft high.'[54]

Curtis also used bulbous and tuberous plants in the garden such as *Sparaxis* and *Ixia viridis*, from South Africa. He describes them and an unidentified clematis from New Zealand which was flowering on bare stems. In the 2003 'Historic Landscape Survey and Restoration Plan' it is suggested that this clematis was *Clematis paniculata lobata*, but this must be incorrect as this plant does not flower on bare stems. Curtis wrote:

> 'For our sparaxis are in bloom and the spikes of Ixia viridis are 18 inches high, I measured one 2 feet. A clematis from New Zealand on the label you sent me has been flowering against the rock for a month past without foliage, a large single whitish flower.'[55]

Other bulbs that were grown at La Chaire included *Amaryllis belladonna, Amaryllis lutea* and *Amaryllis purpurea*. Curtis wrote about them as being in bloom and producing a wonderful display. The conditions at La Chaire were obviously suitable to plants such as *Gladiolus cardinalis* as Curtis wrote that in 1853 he could have cut a thousand blooms from them.[56]

The north side of the garden in the Himalayan glade must have been an impressive site. In another letter to Sir William, Curtis stated that *Rhododendron arboreum* was a beautiful sight and that there were rhododendron hybrids eight feet high that were covered in purple, crimson, and scarlet flowers.[57]

The weather over the years was not always conducive to the plant types Curtis grew, with some years being better than others. The year 1857 was a particularly mild winter during which he wrote about picking flowers for the house the whole length of the winter period, with plants barely checked by cold weather:

> 'For this winter has scarcely injured the foliage of the geraniums on our borders, and there has not been a day in which I could not have gathered roses, and mesembryanthumum. Even the bunches of grapes show themselves on many parts of our rock and house. We have Strawberries larger than pears.'[58]

After Curtis died in 1860 various members of his immediate family lived at La Chaire and maintained the garden. Reports state that the plants put in by him were growing well. In 1871 his grown up children, Harriet, William, and Sarah all resided at La Chaire and were all now in their sixties. In 1877 photographs show that his planting was still immature but thriving.

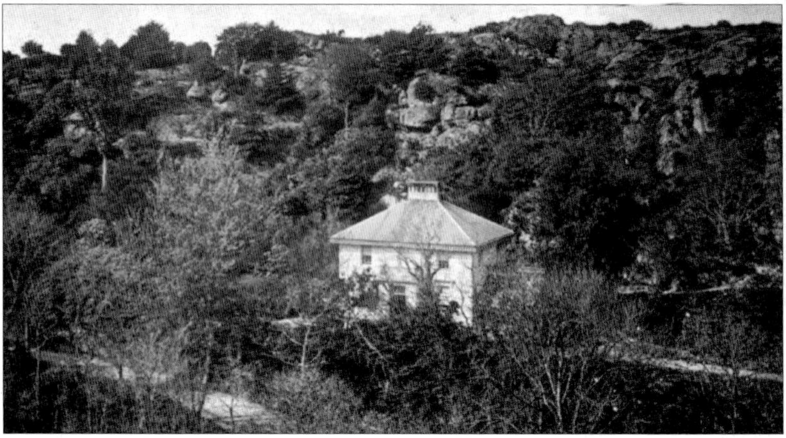

Fig 16 Photograph of La Chaire taken from the north side of the garden in 1877 still showing a degree of plant immaturity, the house clearly seen

Then in 1884 the short-lived publication, *The Jersey Gardener*, published an article on La Chaire which provides an important record of how the garden looked once Curtis's planting had reached maturity.[59] An 1893 photograph shows the planting now completely surrounding the house. A eucalyptus towers at least 80 feet above it.

By the time that this photograph was taken the garden would have looked much as Curtis would have planned and envisaged. The years after his death had not seen any particularly harsh weather so the garden had not suffered unduly. That was to change in 1895 when a devastating blizzard hit La Chaire and destroyed the towering eucalyptus and most of his tropical plants. This marked the end of La Chaire as a tropical garden and by 1898 it had been sold to a new owner named Charles Fletcher, who would radically change the structure and style of the garden.

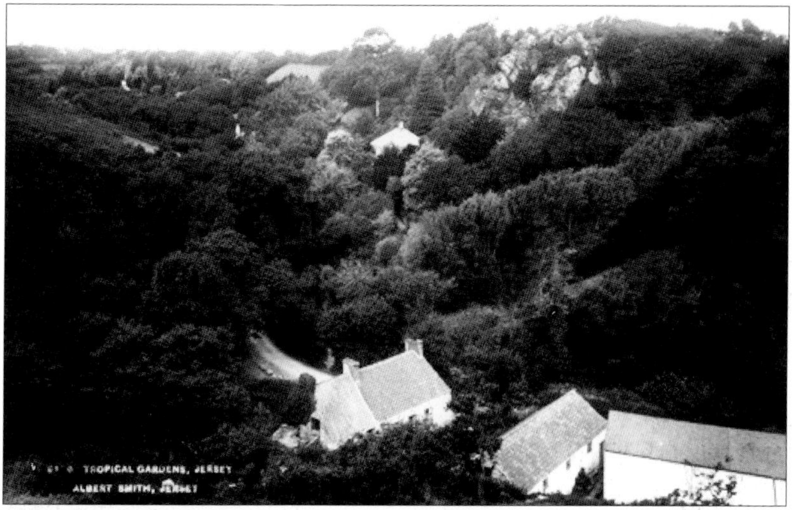

Fig 17 This photograph was taken in 1893 and shows the plants Curtis had acquired are now mature and completely surround the house.

There is one original giant tree that still survives at La Chaire, this was planted during the tenure of Curtis and is a *Cupressus macrocarpa*. The tree had a superficial makeover for the cameras for *More Hidden Gardens*, but the much needed maintenance was left unfinished, and today the tree is in poor condition. The species was introduced around 1838 from America and Curtis was thought to have planted it sometime in 1850, making it one of the first planted in Jersey.[60] There were others planted along the top of the southern valley that formed part of the shelterbelt.

Two other plants survive from the time after Curtis's death and before Fletcher's ownership. These were planted while the property belonged to his daughter Harriet. They can both be found in the garden of Magnolia Cottage, the former head gardener's house. The first, *Eucryphia cordifolia* was introduced from Chile and requires protection in a sheltered position on the mainland. The second is the *Magnolia Campbellii* which was introduced in 1868, eight years after the death of Curtis. This tree is reputed to be the best specimen in Europe.

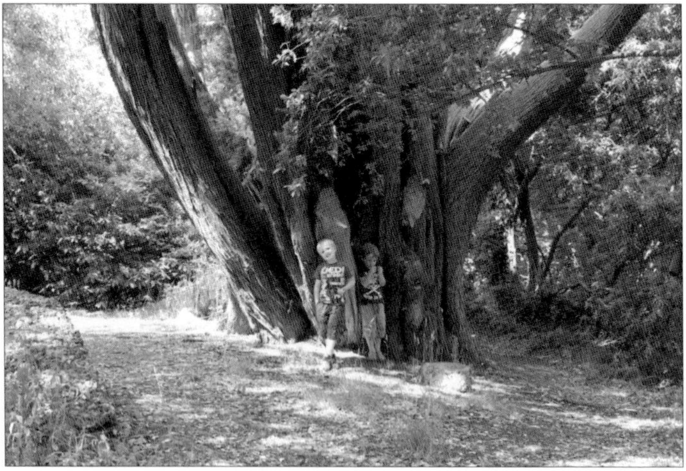

Fig 18 This *Cypress macrocarpa* once formed part of the original shelter belt that was planted by Samuel Curtis around 1850. My two boys give some idea of the size of this tree.

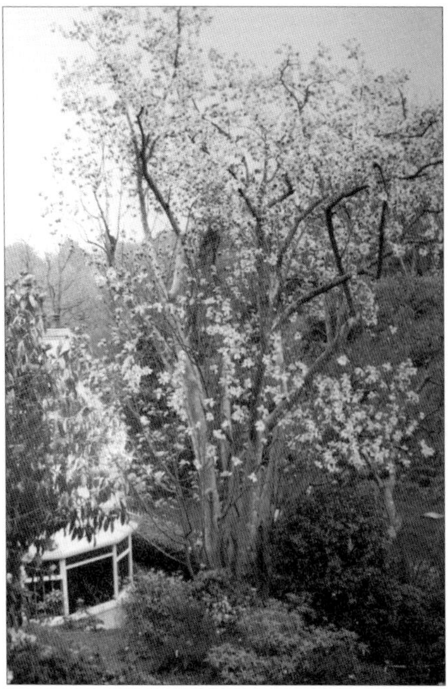

Fig 19 The *Magnolia Campbellii* planted shortly after the death of Samuel Curtis by his daughter Harriet. The tree is in the garden of Magnolia Cottage the former head gardener's cottage and where Fletcher built his 'new' garden much later, before the cottage existed.

~ 5 ~

The 'Cross' of La Chaire

Curtis was a deeply religious and principled man, a committed Quaker. He continued to live according to Quaker philosophy after he was disowned by the Society of Friends. A large rock rising up behind and to the left of the house was used as a look-out position during the Napoleonic wars, before the shelter belt planted by Curtis existed. The rock resembled a pulpit and from here it is said Curtis preached the gospel to his workers toiling away below him, constructing the garden. The rock became known locally as Pulpit Rock, and this name is still used today. Quakers do not preach and proselytise so this is perhaps an exaggeration and that Curtis simply issued instructions from this commanding position, although the erection of a cross in the garden of a religious man would not be unusual.

The exact date of the photograph (Fig 21) is unknown but can be narrowed down. The cross was still in position in 1897 when Charles Fletcher bought La Chaire. It stood looking out towards France, facing east, and would have been visible to passing ships. Fletcher makes reference to it in diary entries on more than one occasion. He enjoyed photography and took many pictures of the garden, so this photograph could have been taken by him.

In his diary entry for Monday 1st May, 1899, Fletcher discusses moving some bamboo from immediately around the cross, bamboo that would have been planted by Curtis.[61] There is no bamboo visible around it in Fig 21 so the photograph had to have been taken after this date. Fletcher wrote: 'Today we got on really well with the planting. Planted the 6 nobilis bamboos from the cross about the waterfall where they look very well.'[62] Other possible dates for the photograph of the cross could be either Friday 1st June, 1906 or Saturday

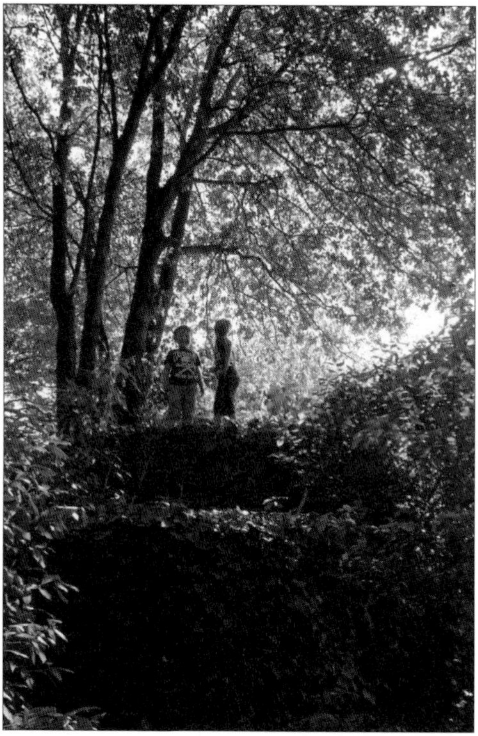

Left: Fig 20 This photograph shows the pulpit rock at La Chaire. The two boys standing where Curtis once surveyed his garden and directed his workforce.

Below: Fig 21 The photograph shows the Cross of La Chaire. The date of this photograph is unknown but was taken sometime between 1st May, 1899 and 11th July, 1906.

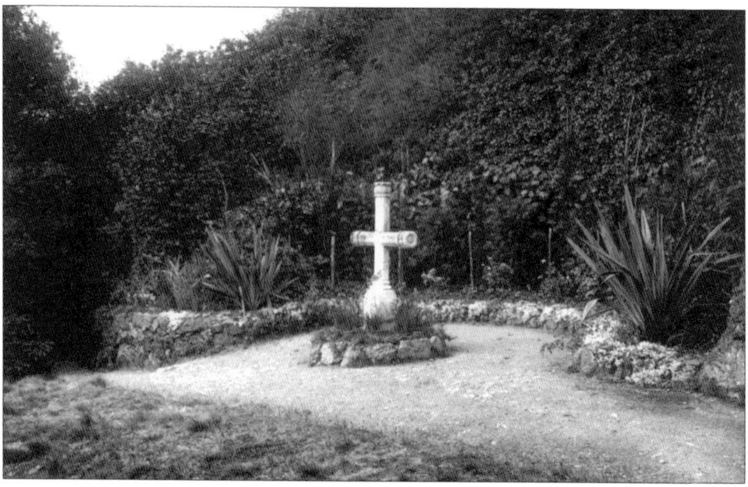

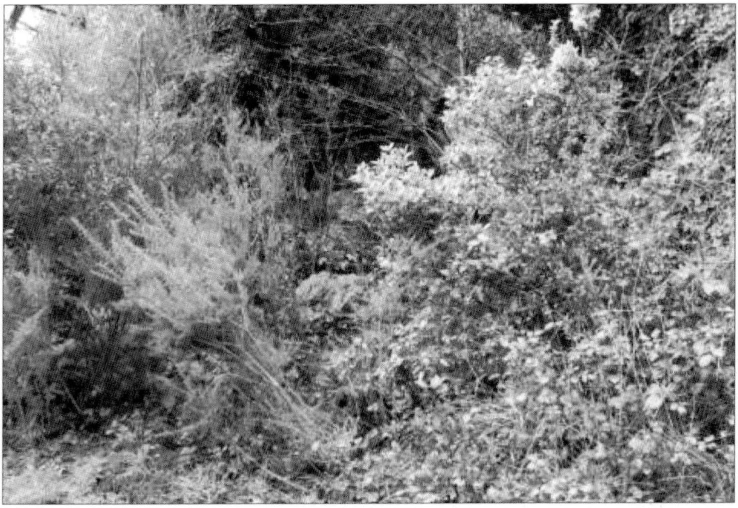

Fig 22 The photograph shows the old position of the cross at La Chaire, taken in 2012. The stones that denote the boundary as seen in fig 21 are still in the original position as are the stones that the cross stands on.

2nd June, 1906. A Jersey photographer named Albert Smith, who over many years took literally thousands of pictures of Jersey scenes and everyday life for such things as postcards, arrived at La Chaire to photograph the garden. He was rained off on the Friday but came back the next day to complete the session.

The plants around the cross in Fig 21 can be identified as *Phormium tenax*. In another diary entry for 22nd September, 1903, Fletcher writes about planting New Zealand flax around the garden, so the planting was possibly from this date.[63] In the photograph the flax looks large and established, so there is a strong possibility it was planted in 1903 and was photographed in 1906. The picure could be attributed to either Fletcher or Smith.[64]

Fletcher obviously enjoyed the cross as a feature and made sure that it was planted up well. He wrote that he planned to plant violets there. This was one relic from the time of Curtis that Fletcher kept very much as it had always been, just changing the planting design around it. He wrote: 'The gardeners today prepared a violet bed at the cross....I also wrote to Veitch for 3 dozen plants of Violets.'[65]

The cross is carved from oolitic limestone, which is not indigenous to Jersey and so would have been imported. Limestone is found in France around Caen so this would be its most likely provenance.

There are no records of what happened to the cross, and until recently it had disappeared and was thought lost. That was until the cross arm was found in a local garden. From this piece, and using the original photograph (Fig 21) it is possible to calculate the exact dimensions of the entire feature.

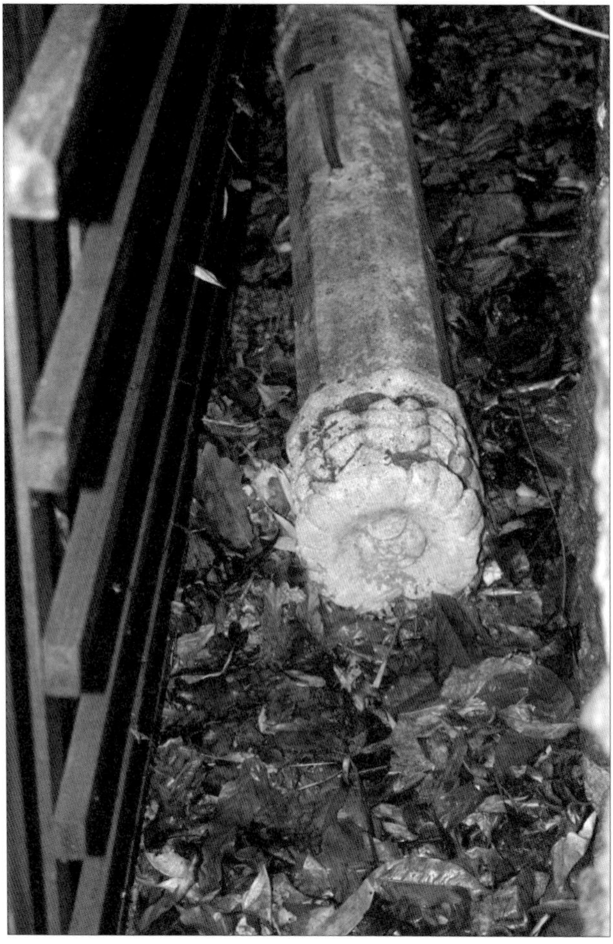

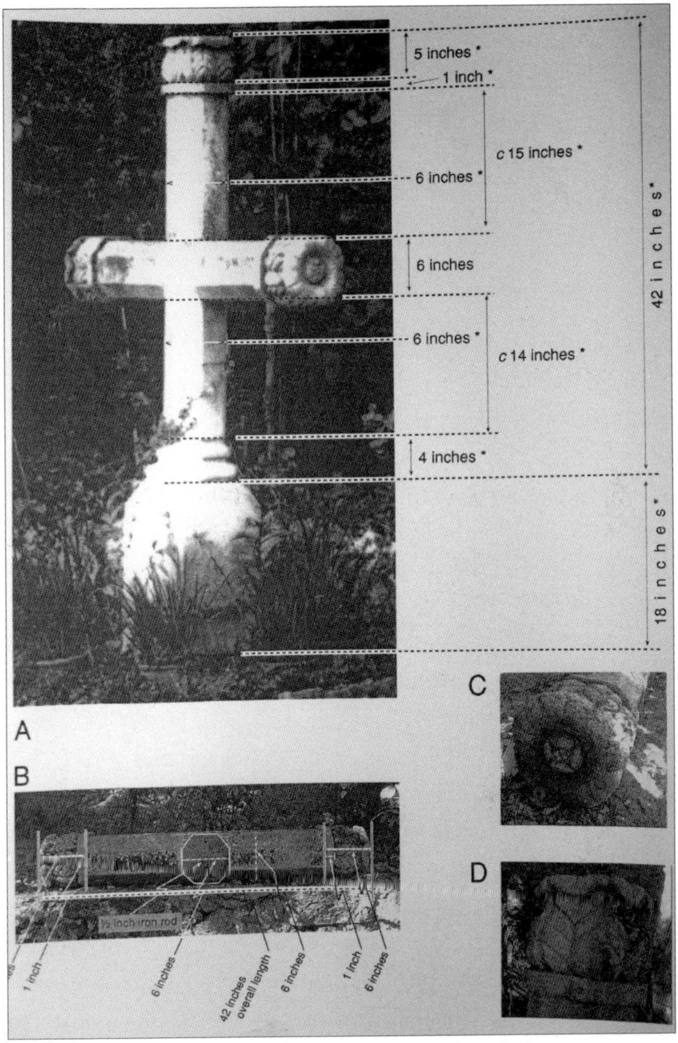

Fig 24 The exact dimensions of the cross at La Chaire can be seen in this illustration. The size calculations ascertained from the discovered arm. This was a main feature of the garden while under the ownership of Curtis and Fletcher. The plans to restore the garden included using the original arm but re-carving the rest in the same limestone and putting it back in the original position.

~ 6 ~

New owner Charles Fletcher

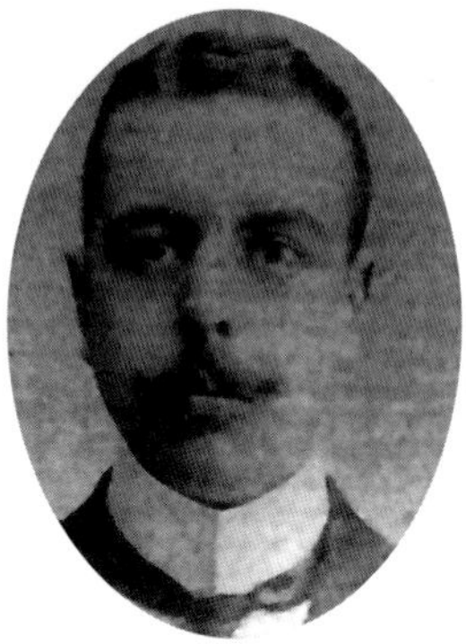

In 1861, a year after the death of Samuel Curtis, his widowed daughter, Mrs Harriet Fothergill, was the only person residing at La Chaire. By 1871, census returns show that she had been joined by her brother William and sister Sarah.[66] Then, on 19th March 1883, Sarah died at the age of 70. William was next, dying on 28th February, 1887 at the aged 83. William had collected plants for his father and for a time had a nursery in Margate in north-east Kent. For the second time Harriet lived alone at La Chaire until she died on 15th August 1888, at the age of 81. Harriet had been a widow for much of her adult life and a companion to her father.

La Chaire was inherited by Harriet's niece, Mrs Phebe Rooke, a widow who retained the property until she sold it to Charles Fletcher in April 1898. Rooke lived at La Chaire during her period of ownership, but also briefly leased the property in 1896 to Her Royal Highness Princess Victoria Kaiulani of Hawaii.

The sale negotiations between Rooke and Fletcher were protracted. She refused the initial offers made by him to purchase La Chaire from her. Fletcher made his first approaches through the Jersey firm Le Gallais who were then and still are estate agents. He began the year 1898 by over-wintering at the Hotel Metropole, Monte Carlo, but by the end of January he and his wife had crossed the border into Italy and were staying in Bordighera when Fletcher resumed the sale negotiations. In a diary entry for Monday 31st January, 1898, he was despondent and wrote: 'Received a letter from Le Gallais today who says that La Chaire is not to be sold.'[67] He started to consider buying another property in Jersey called Rockmount House in Bouley Bay, which today would sell for around £2 million. But, on 5th February, Fletcher received another letter informing him that Le Gallais had contacted Rooke again and had asked her to reconsider the decision not to sell. Rooke obviously acquiesced as in a diary entry for Friday 11th February, he wrote: 'Received a letter from Benest. As far as I can make out I shall probably buy La Chaire for about £2,000.'[68] Acquiring La Chaire for £2,000 was a short-lived hope as, on Friday 18th February, he received another letter from Benest informing him that Rooke would not sell for less than £3,000.[69] Finally and after three more letters, news arrived that La Chaire was to be his. Fletcher was happy and in a diary entry for Thursday 3rd March he wrote: 'Lovely day. I wrote to Benest telling him I would give £3,000 for La Chaire but insisted on possession by April 11.'[70]

On 19th April 1898, Fletcher, now back in Jersey handed a cheque for £3,000 to E. B. Renouf and La Chaire came into his ownership. Fletcher must have been using the Jersey Ecrivain (Solicitor) Snowdon Benest as can be seen from his diary entries, but he gave the purchase cheque to the solicitor E. B. Renouf. Records cannot be found to ascertain whether Renouf was employed by Benest or if Fletcher employed both men. The most likely scenario is that Renouf worked for Le Gallais who were instrumental in the sale. Neither men were engaged by Phebe Rooke as she was not officially represented but was being advised by a trusted neighbour during the sale.

Charles Fletcher was born into a wealthy landowning family in 1870. They resided at Dale Park, Madehurst, in West Sussex. Charles stood on his father's death to inherit the family estate and fortune, but this did not happen as he died before his father. He had also been disinherited before his death. The disinheritance occurred because Fletcher met and married a woman named Ethel Beddoes.

Ethel worked as a Gaiety Girl. These were respectable women, being chorus girls at the Gaiety Theatre, London. They danced beautifully and wore the latest fashions, unlike the burlesque dancers prevalent at that time who did not wear much at all. Fletcher was possibly one of the rich aristocrats who would wait outside the Gaiety stage door for the girls to come out so he could take them to dinner. Some of these girls married into society and the Gaiety stage door became a popular meeting place. Alan Hyman in his book makes reference to this: 'At the old Gaiety in the Strand the chorus was becoming a matrimonial agency for girls with ambitions to marry into the peerage.'[71] Fletcher's surviving family members do not believe that he frequented the Gaiety stage door. They believe he was a man who saw Ethel, fell in love with her, and then married her. They say he did not make a habit of escorting young pretty dancers. Fletcher's family did not approve of Ethel, not because she was a Gaiety dancer – other young Gaiety Girls had after all married into society – although this would not have made her an ideal candidate for a daughter-in-law. The insurmountable barrier for them accepting her was that she had an illegitimate son. This fact they could not and would not accept. Fletcher disregarded his parent's refusal to allow their marriage and they became man and wife on 27th February 1895. The marriage proposal had led to an ultimatum from Fletcher's parents. They left him in no doubt that if he persisted in the relationship he would be cut off from them, and would forfeit his inheritance. He was cut off, but offered £64,000 as a one-off payment on the understanding that he would receive not a penny more, and that Ethel would never set foot at Dale. Fletcher was not happy but he did accept the offer, not allowing his pride to stand in the way of what now would amount to around two and a half million pounds. This act demonstrates a love and commitment for Ethel that far outweighed money and his birthright as the eldest son. In effect he turned his back on a vast fortune as the money he accepted was a tiny fraction of what he could have expected to inherit.

Charley (Ethel's son) never lived with his mother for any length of time but was brought up by two aunts. He was educated at The Cathedral School, Hereford, and even though he must have missed his mother very much, he was loved and adored by his aunts. He did at times holiday at La Chaire, playing with his half-brother, the son of his mother, Ethel, and her new husband. Their son was also named Charles – Charles Hugh Fletcher. Throughout Fletcher's diaries, his son was referred to by name only a few times. He was constantly called baby or, instead, the boy.

Charley Fairlie Cunningham became in reality a family secret. Many years

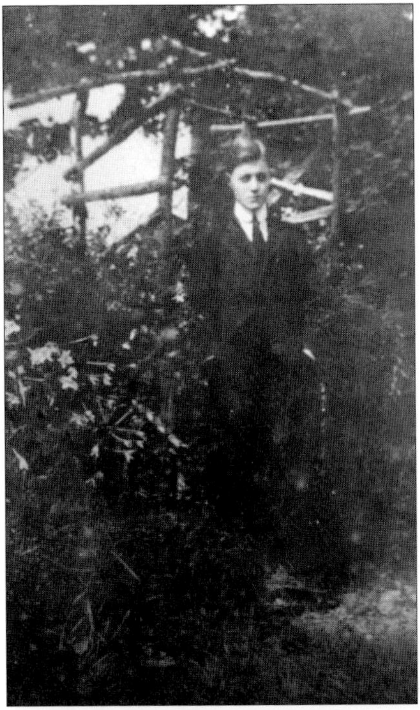

Left: Fig 25 Ethel's Beddoes first (illegitimate) son was named Charley Fairlie Cunningham after his father. He was brought up by his mother's aunts and sadly became a family secret.

Below: Fig 26 The photographs show Ethel and Dora Barks, aunts of Ethel who brought up Charley her son. They lived in a Queen Anne house in Ascot which can still be seen from the stands at Ascot racecourse.

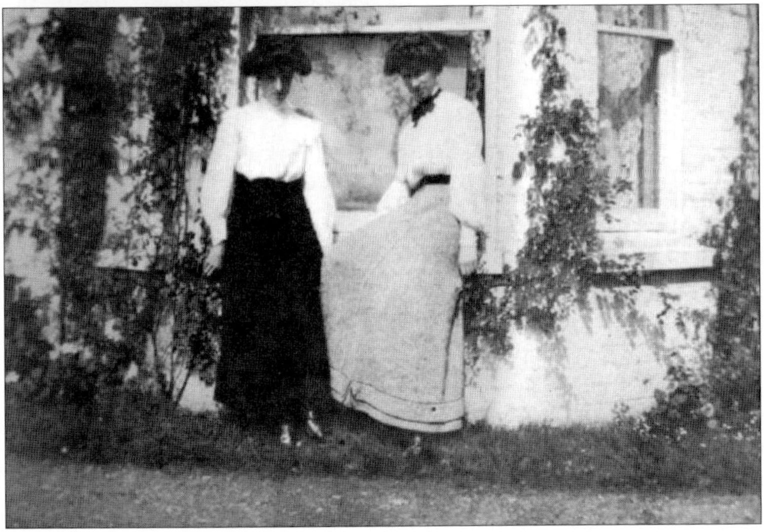

later family members did not even know of his existence. Fletcher's son, Charles Hugh, married and had a daughter named Sarah; she was never told about Charlie. Sarah explained this:

> I think the shame and disgrace, the dark secret. Poor Charley, he was a dear good funny man. Charley is Charlie Fairlie Cunningham, Ethel's son by Sir Charles Fairlie Cunningham, about six years older than my father. He became an actor, I always imagine him in plays where he would burst through the French doors saying anyone for tennis. I was totally unaware of his existence until I was about 30. He died in a council flat in Islington, in about 1980, so sad.[72]

Fletcher's son later inherited La Chaire before selling it in 1921. He never visited La Chaire again, but he did at times stay with his grandparents at Dale. Blood ties were obviously strong. They still wanted to see their grandchild even though he was from a daughter-in-law they despised. He became a Captain in the Rifles and fought bravely with distinction at the Somme. His life after the Great War was scarred by the horror he witnessed and experienced, like so many other brave men. The futile waste of life that he witnessed stayed with him and he would have bouts of depression for the rest of his life. Even though he was too old to be posted abroad, he served his country again in the Second World War, but was based in England. Sarah never heard her father talk about his mother Ethel, her grandmother, but he did talk about his father. Sarah remembers one story that he used to tell her about his life at La Chaire:

> My father used to tell me the story of the wooden peg sailor doll. My father adored my grandfather and used to walk around the garden with him. Whenever they got to this particularly big tree my grandfather would throw this wooden peg doll dressed as a sailor up into it and they would watch it bump its way back down, hitting each branch. He always enjoyed watching this. Then one day the doll got stuck and did not come back down. Maybe it's still stuck up there.[73]

The bouts of depression suffered by Charles Hugh Fletcher may have been passed down in the genes from his father, Charles. In an entry for Friday, 15th September, 1899, Fletcher makes reference to feeling depressed while at La

Chaire and it is not the only entry that alludes to this state of mind. Fletcher wrote about Jersey: 'This place is too damnably dull for words and I feel very depressed.'[74]

All through his diaries a steady picture builds up of the large amount of alcohol Fletcher was consuming on a daily basis. Hardly a day would go by without a good lunch and accompanying wine or spirits being served. This dangerously high intake had an extremely detrimental effect on his health. Fletcher recorded (sometimes indirectly) in his diaries on a month-by-month and year-by-year basis his worsening health, writing 'feeling seedy today' – his words for feeling unwell. As the recorded diary years go by, from 1898 to 1906 the 'feeling seedy' description is increasingly used. His diaries end abruptly in July 1906 but it is known that he became ill and arrived in London under the care of doctors. He refused the use of his parents' London home and rented a flat. He was in fact dying of cirrhosis of the liver. This and exhaustion was recorded on his death certificate as the cause of death. Fletcher died on 18th November, 1907, at the young age of 36.

Ethel was treated shamefully by her husband's family. She was given no say in the funeral arrangements and when she went to Dale for the service was refused entry at the main door. Instruction had been left that she was to use the servant's entrance. The family completely ignored Ethel and she was told to leave the house as soon as the funeral was over. Ethel's life spiralled downwards after Fletcher's death. She married a man who was an alcoholic, living with him in Brighton. It is said that they both died from the effects of alcohol. Ethel became just a footnote in the history of La Chaire.

Fletcher was buried in an unmarked grave by his family and not placed in the family plot. He had disgraced them and his punishment continued even after his death. Sarah, his granddaughter, went to find the grave around thirty years ago but could not locate it until she asked a lady arranging flowers in the church if she knew where he might lay. This lady had in fact been a housemaid at Dale Park and knew the exact location of the grave. She said how sad it was how he and Ethel had been treated. Fletcher still remains in an unmarked grave and most likely always will.

In the restoration project material Charles Fletcher was referred to as a playboy and a Toad of Toad Hall-like figure. His family dislike the playboy epithet but this is undeniably what he was. The term should not be understood as derogatory, but Fletcher was a man of independent means, he never had to seek employment and spent months of the year touring France and Italy. He stayed at all the best hotels and frequented many casinos. This was just the life he led and the life into which he had been born. The Toad of Toad Hall comparison is not particularly pleasant and could be construed as derogatory, but there are similarities in character between Toad and Fletcher. Fletcher always desired to have the best that money could buy. He purchased items on a whim without any consultation with his wife.

At times this caused Ethel a deal of consternation. He first of all spent a large amount of money on a yacht called *Wayward* which they sailed back and forth between the English mainland, France and Jersey. Later, after spending a large sum of money on its purchase and subsequent upgrade, he sold *Wayward* and bought a variety of horse-drawn carriages of the latest designs. Next he purchased a motor car, the first in Jersey. He dashed around the Island at an alarming speed, spending a fortune having the car repaired after its many breakdowns and his improvements to it. The main problem he encountered was finding somewhere to purchase petrol on the Island as no one sold it. He did not stay with one car but bought and sold a number of them. Unlike Toad he did not purchase an aeroplane but had he lived longer he may very well have done so.

Having permanently settling in Jersey, a constant in Fletcher's life, apart from his love of Ethel, was the garden of La Chaire. He may have jumped between yachts, carriages and cars but La Chaire remained foremost He never lost interest in the house or the garden and was always focused on their progress and completion.

While they were travelling abroad Fletcher would make notes in his diaries about different gardens they had visited. He would note names of plants and plant groupings that he thought would work well at La Chaire. He would always enjoy the gardens of good hotels and exotic gardens in the south of France and Italy. On 18th February 1898, while staying in Bordighera, Italy, he wrote in his diary:

> 'We drove after luncheon to Mrs Hanbury's gardens known as La Mortola, a really lovely place. Magnificent gardens most picturesquely situated sloping down to the sea and an extremely picturesque house. I wish we had time to go again.[75]

La Mortola became the major inspiration in Fletcher's designs for La Chaire, giving him ideas as to what he could achieve. Both layouts were very similar, being coastal and woodland gardens. Thomas Hanbury in 1869 employed the German botanist Ludwig Winter to design and develop La Mortola. Like La Chaire, La Mortola was on a slope; it included steps, pathways, pools and moving water. La Mortola with its rare and exotic plants became a blueprint for what Fletcher later achieved at La Chaire. In January 1899 both Fletcher and Ethel were back in Bordighera and revisited La Mortola. His diary entry for Monday 23rd January shows that he was seeking ideas for planting at La Chaire:

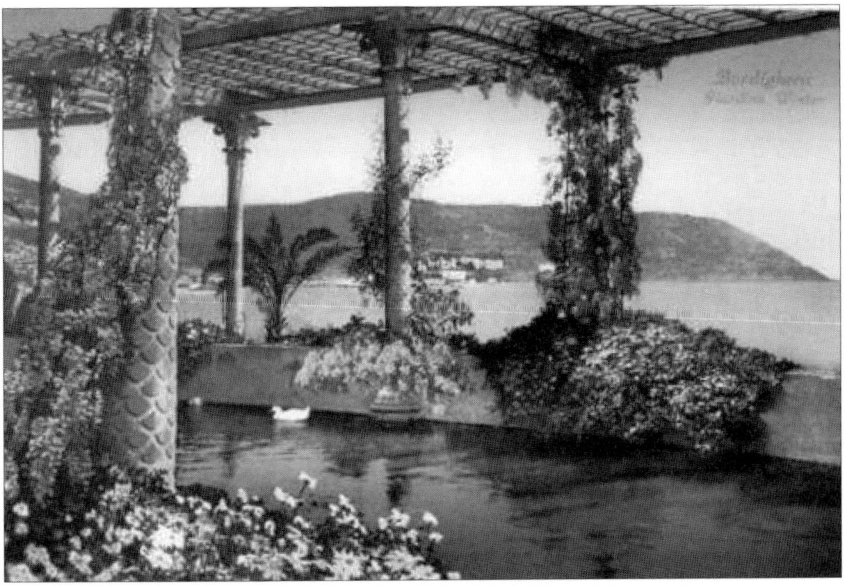

Fig 27 This postcard shows Ludwig Winter's garden at Bordighera, Italy

> 'This afternoon Ethel and I drove to La Mortola. The gardens will of course look prettier a little later on but they are very fine. I made a note of several striking trees and plants that might do at La Chaire. They only have common varieties of bamboo at La Mortola but mitis has grown to a gigantic size.'[76]

Fletcher and Ethel also visited Winter's Palm Garden in Bordighera, the garden designed by Ludwig Winter after he had finished working for Thomas Hanbury. Winter specialised in Palms and introduced them to the region. La Chaire was later to have palms raised by Winter from his Bordighera garden and nursery – one is still growing there today.

Fletcher employed builders and gardeners to construct his house and grounds and he displayed a keenness to have the work completed as soon as possible. This led to him having greater expectations than may have been reasonable. He desired instant effect from the builders and gardeners and would not suffer fools gladly, sacking anyone whom he thought was not working as hard or as well as he considered they should be. There were undoubtedly occasions when he was correct but from the diaries it does seem that he could antagonise people.

Fletcher made an entry in his 1899 diary concerning his builder Springate, who did seem to be getting on with the tasks well, but obviously not quickly enough. Fletcher records that he rowed with Springate about how fast the work was progressing. He displayed a general impatience with the progression both inside and out. A demonstration of how Fletcher could antagonise and not elicit the best out of people can be seen from another diary entry he made in 1899. There is the possibility that Fletcher was behaving justly, but he was likely conscious of the fact that he may have been perceived as someone to be parted from his money for as long as it was possible to do so. He suspected and accused Springate of dawdling to extend the work and make more money.

So long after the event Fletcher's true character has to be subject to conjecture, but it is perhaps realistic to assume that he thought of himself as a target for the unscrupulous and was being perceived as a rich man who had more money than sense. To dispel this he simply displayed his authority the only way he knew how. Fletcher was not averse to sacking workers if he felt it necessary and he would do this without warning.

Fletcher had a neighbour named William Walton who lived just a little way up the valley from La Chaire in a house called La Rive. The two men had a turbulent relationship. Walton, or Old Walton as Fletcher called him, owned land that adjoined La Chaire at its western edge. Walton also owned land that lay directly opposite La Chaire where he had sole rights to the narrow stream. They disagreed about access to the stream and some of the work being undertaken by Fletcher's builders. Walton became obstinate and bent on thwarting Fletcher's plans whenever he could. Fletcher did at times try to persuade Walton to cooperate whenever possible.

The main bone of contention centred on access and rights to the stream. Fletcher wanted to run La Chaire's garden waste water drains into it. Although Walton resided higher up the valley on the same side as La Chaire, he owned a narrow strip of land opposite Fletcher and a larger amount of land below him, again on the opposite side of the road with the stream running through it. Walton refused to allow the garden drains of La Chaire to be run into the stream as he said that he would be greatly inconvenienced by having to get his water for this lower land, higher up, above the proposed drains. Walton must have needed the clean water as he was growing fruit and vegetables and possibly keeping some animals. He had built a boathouse in the harbour but it is doubtful that he was taking water from the stream for this because of the distance between the two. Negotiations for access were conducted through Fletcher's solicitor, but they broke down and in a diary entry for October 1900, Fletcher wrote:

> 'We drove into town and E. B. Renouf lunched with us at the Hotel de L' Europe. We talked over what we were to do about old Walton and have decided once and for all to cut him off absolutely.'[77]

Later the next month Fletcher wrote that the builders had been able to come up with a solution to the drains issue without being under any obligation to Walton.

Another issue arose from a large tree that was growing on Walton's strip of land in front of La Chaire. The tree blocked out light and Fletcher wanted it removed, but Walton refused point blank to allow any work on it at all. However he did offer to sell the strip of land the tree was on for £1 thousand, knowing that this was a gross exaggeration of the real value. Eventually Renouf his solicitor heard from Walton to say that he was now open to an offer for the strip of land. Today this land is still part of the La Rive estate, and does not belong to La Chaire, so it is unlikely that Fletcher did succeed in buying it. Later that month Fletcher spoke to Walton face to face about the tree and he agreed to allow some branches to be removed. Fletcher noted in his diary: 'Saw old Walton about lopping the branches of the big tree. He appeared fairly agreeable.'[78]

Fletcher also wished to buy a field from the local farmer Charles Renouf that in a diary entry he states was next to La Chaire, between him and Walton. A section of this field must also have been opposite as in January 1902 Fletcher wrote: 'We cut down Renouf's tree opposite La Chaire which lets in more light.'[79] There is difficulty in understanding whether Fletcher meant that this land was next to La Rive, Walton's home, or next to the land Walton owned below La Chaire. Land has been bought and sold all around the area during the hundred-plus years since Fletcher's tenure. The farming family Renouf do still own land that goes down the northern valley slope to La Chaire so it may have been bought back by them, or Fletcher for whatever reason never in the end purchased it. What is certain, from the lack of light Fletcher comments on, is that the trees around the garden had grown so large that they seemed to be closing in on the house.

One sentence in a diary entry, not about Walton but another person he considered was being difficult, sums up the many problems and lack of understanding Fletcher had with his neighbours, his gardeners and builders. He wrote, 'I shall never understand a Jerseyman'.

As the years from 1898 to 1906 go by it becomes evident from the diary entries and the general tone of Fletcher's writing that there is a lack of money, and that this is becoming a worry to him. His health is also deteriorating as from the September to the end of October 1902 he is suffering from bouts of giddiness caused by liver problems, brought on by his heavy drinking. He made an entry regarding the garden in August 1902, but then hardly gave it a mention until April 1903. His diary entries become sparse and short, he constantly writes that he is bored to death. The reason seems to be that a lack of funds, illness and depression along with a tangible fear that he would be drafted into the Jersey Militia were all weighing heavily on his mind. Because of the Boer War Jersey introduced conscription into the militia. His diaries constantly focus on the militia problem which played a large part in his general state of mind. From his diaries it does appear that one or two people in authority enjoyed the worry and discomfiture that this caused him. The first months of 1903 still see him in a depressed state. In medical terms liver problems can bring about the side effect of depression.

To provide funds to build the house and garden Fletcher raised loans from the bank on his capital, the idea being to leave his capital untouched and pay back the loans from interest accrued. But he was spending large amounts of money and estimated costs of his projects invariably ran over-budget. By December 1902 the bank had increased his loan to £22,000, but interest raised on his securities was not keeping pace with the required repayments. In 1906 money problems are constant and feature regularly in his diary. Fletcher in the same month was due to pay a bill received from the Veitch Nursery but he was forced to write to them and ask them to wait until June for payment. He simply did not have the available funds to hand. At this time the diaries highlight chronic signs of liver disease, this being just a year before his drinking killed him.

~ 7 ~

Charles Fletcher tranforms La Chaire

Even before 19th April 1898, when La Chaire officially became his, Fletcher was making plans for the house and garden. As far back as early March he had written to the Gorey builders, Springate and Baal, about demolishing Curtis's house, and building a new one in its place. While he was in Grasse, France, in March, he sent his friend in Jersey (a man called Parish) to meet with Springate and Baal to discuss all the possibilities and ideas regarding La Chaire. By the beginning of April, again before La Chaire was his, Fletcher's builders were surveying the property and reported that there would be great difficulties in building the foundations for a new house. With this in mind Fletcher decided to build onto the existing house instead.

He employed the Jersey architect Adolp Curry to draw up the construction plans. For the remainder of 1898 Fletcher made many visits to La Chaire, always arriving by horse and carriage or bicycle. He did not reside there with Ethel until 1st January, 1899. Soon after that they left for London and then to Italy to overwinter in the sun, arriving at Bordighera on 16th January. The house was being radically changed in their absence from the simple abode that Curtis had built, into a far larger and more impressive residence. It was from these alterations that La Chaire took the name Chateau La Chaire. Fletcher detailed the changes:

> 'Blowing a gale. Left La Chaire and went to The Grand to get an early start tomorrow. Left La Chaire in an awful state owing to the workmen who are putting on a new roof, two new bedrooms at back and offices, a smoking room in the place of the old conservatory, a veranda along the front and one side of the house and a terrace with steps up in front. Also there is a certain amount of internal work to be done in the old part of the house.[8]

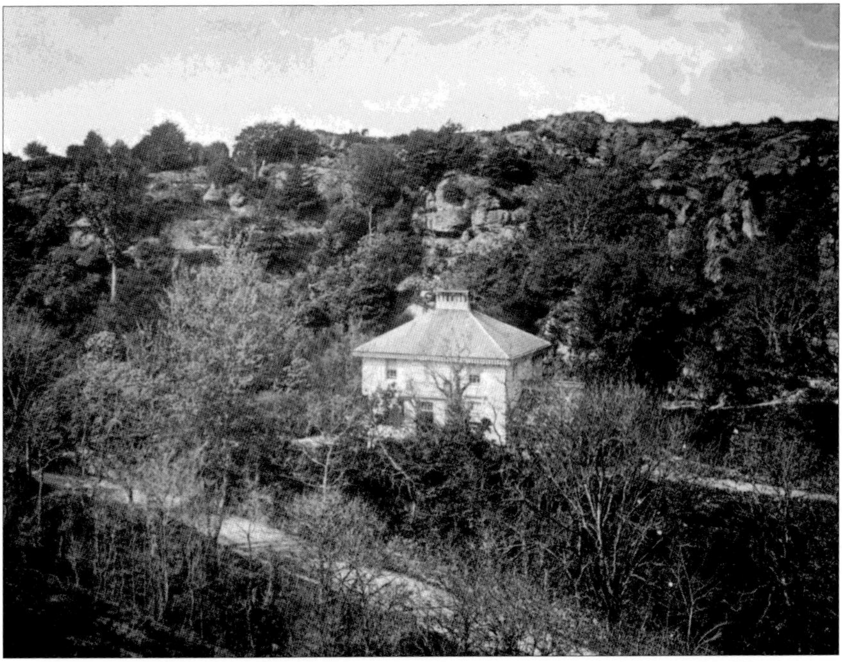

Fig 28 The original property built by Samuel Curtis. At first Curtis named it Rozel Cottage. The photograph shows the steep-sided garden, long before it was fully terraced by Fletcher. The path leading to the house is narrow and there is no real terrace. Fletcher pushed back the cliff face and extended his new house backwards into it. After Fletcher had extended the house he put in a driveway that linked to the road to the left of the building.

Fletcher's new house would occupy his thoughts from now on. There were decisions to be made about the oak panelling of the smoking room and selecting the fireplace most suitable for it, as well as the purchase of carpets and wallpaper, picked out at Hampton's in Pall Mall.

En route to Bordighera in 1899 Fletcher and Ethel stopped off in London and while there visited Kew by train. Fletcher's favourite plant was the bamboo; he would make note of the different species he saw wherever he travelled. Different bamboo species would have prominent positions at La Chaire. Some of the bamboos that he had admired and noted the names of at Kew were later planted in the garden. He recorded this visit:

> … and then trained to Kew. Went over the bamboo garden was most struck with Bamboo *palmata veitchii* and *Phyllostachys viridi glaucescens*. The last had grown to a good height. Nitida was very pretty. Afterwards went over to palm house.[81]

On arrival in Bordighera Fletcher made constant references in his diary to plants that he had seen and thought would be suitable for his garden. On the morning of 18th January he walked to see the Scheffel palms and in the afternoon visited Ludwig Winter's palm nursery to discuss with him the plants he would like to purchase for La Chaire.[82] The next day, 19th January, Fletcher and Ethel were back at Winter's where he measured a large clump of *Phyllostachys mitis* to check the space that this plant would take up in his garden. On 20th January, he was once again in discussion with Winter regarding plant selection. He was making sure that the plants he selected would thrive in Jersey and there was nobody better to advise him than Ludwig Winter. On 26th January 1899 Fletcher had come to a decision on the plants he wanted, and placed an order. He wrote about this in his diary:

> 'This afternoon went to the town and arranged about palms with Winter. Made appointments with him for Monday next.
>
> Ordered 6 *Brahea roezlii*
> 3 *Phoenix canariensis* (large)
> 3 *Phoenix sylvestris* (large)
> 6 *Phoenix australis* (low)'[83]

The reason for arranging to go back to see Winter on the Monday was to select the actual plants he wanted, and also to order other plant types that would be shipped to Jersey. On 30th January he again recorded his dealing with Winter at the nursery:

> 'This afternoon I went down to Winter's and chose the palms etc for La Chaire. A really fine lot. Also bought some agaves, cactus, orange and lemon trees. These ought to improve the appearance of the place enormously.'[84]

Once Fletcher had selected his plants he went to view and photograph them before shipping. With the extra plants he had bought this made a large collection of tropical and exotic specimens. Fletcher wrote about the latest visit to Winter's and recorded the extra plants that he purchased:

> '...went down to Winter's garden to see all the palms etc put together that I have bought from him. A very fine lot. Gave him a cheque on account for £36. Ordered in addition 12 more aloes of different sorts and 4 plants of *Bourgainvilla spectabilis*.'[85]

Whilst in Italy Fletcher was also communicating by letter with two nurseries in England, named Veitch and Gauntlett. Both of these nurseries would later supply plants for La Chaire. The Veitch Nursery operated from its Chelsea base and became the largest family-owned nursery in Europe. It was responsible for the introduction of countless new plant genera and species sent back from all over the world by the plant-hunters they employed. Gauntlett was a Surrey nursery based in Chiddingfold. They produced beautifully illustrated catalogues and supplied a wide range of plants. Fletcher was communicating with them on what he was intending to order and enquiring regarding the support they could offer in the planting process. As well as communicating with the nurseries Fletcher was in constant discussion, again by letter, with his builder Springate. Work at La Chaire was on the whole progressing well.

Of all the palms and other plants that Fletcher ordered from Ludwig Winter only one still remains at La Chaire, this being one of the three *Phoenix canariensis*. Fletcher purchased these plants on 26th January, 1899. They were shipped to Jersey and, apart from the cacti and agaves which arrived a day later, the palms were delivered to La Chaire on Tuesday 25th April. Fletcher and his gardeners planted them out on 1st May. Fletcher recorded this: '... put out the palms from Winter in the pockets near house and around the old eucalyptus stumps...'[86]

Figs 29 and 30 below below are taken from the same position, the first in January 2014 and the second a short time after the Second World War when the chateau had been converted into a hotel. Both photographs show a *Phoenix canariensis* in exactly the same position. This palm is undoubtedly one of Fletcher's plantings. The pocket that contains this palm is very small, in fact too small for a plant that can potentially grow very large. The pocket is packed full of roots and because of this some have had to run along the surface of the surrounding rock to try to find soil elsewhere. For a plant of this age it might be expected that by 2014 it would be far larger, but it has been kept smaller by its confinement and most of the trees around are also smaller than might otherwise be expected. This is due to the prevailing wind.

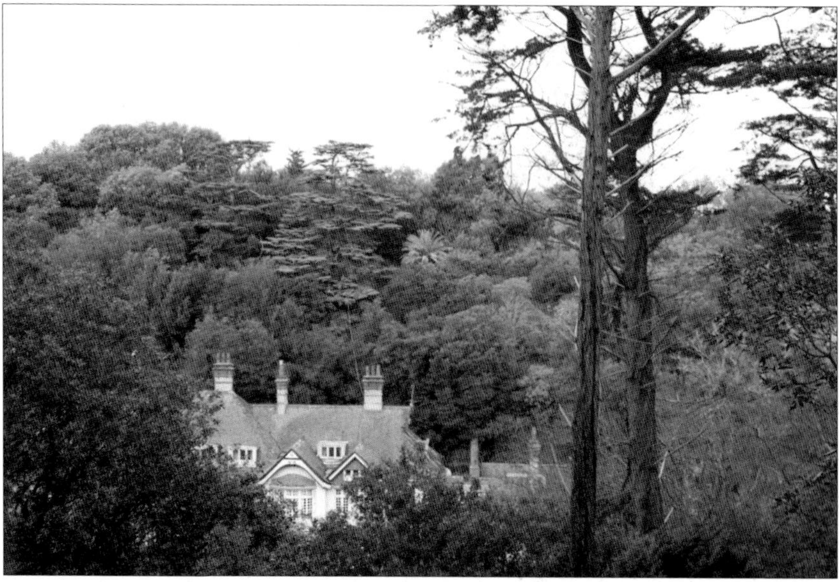

Fig 29 Just to the right of the last main chimney on the right, on the main building and near the top of the garden, can be seen the fronds of the *Phoenix canariensis*

Fletcher also wanted plants for the terrace so he purchased for shipping back to Jersey a range of containers. To hold the lemon and orange trees he paid £76 for four copper and brass Louis XVI palm pots and two silver pots that bore the coat of arms of Cardinal Richelieu. He bought these from an antique dealer in Bordighera. By 14th March 1899, both he and Ethel had arrived in Monte Carlo where he again purchased more containers for the garden – a dozen terracotta pots that would go on the terrace walls.

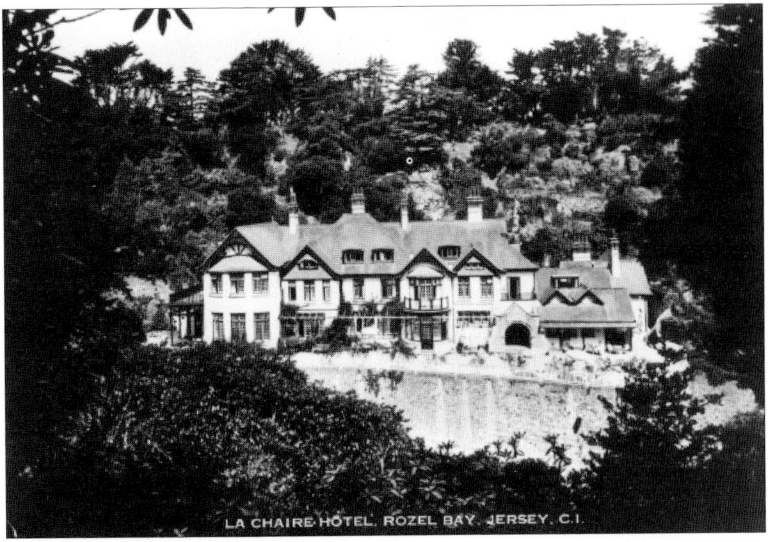

Fig 30 In the same position as the photograph above the *Phoenix canariensis* can be seen.

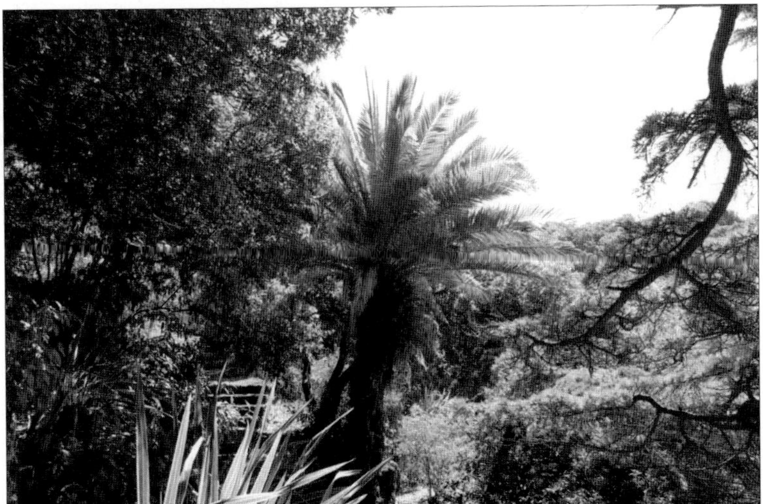

Fig 31 The *Phoenix canariensis* which was planted by Charles Fletcher in 1899. This plant is still in its original planting pocket.

Whilst not in Jersey Fletcher was constantly thinking about La Chaire and was in communication with a company called Graham & Banks, from whom he ordered two sets of entrance gates. These gates are still in place today, but he did not like the set that face the harbour, as he wrote that they looked too low for the archway.

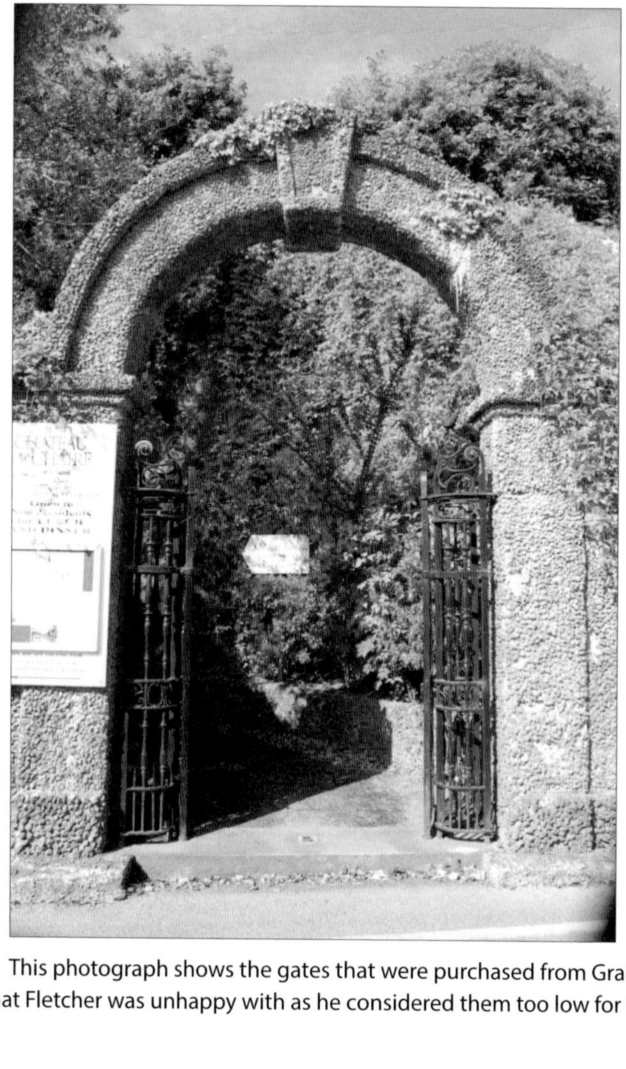

Fig 32 This photograph shows the gates that were purchased from Graham & Banks that Fletcher was unhappy with as he considered them too low for the arch

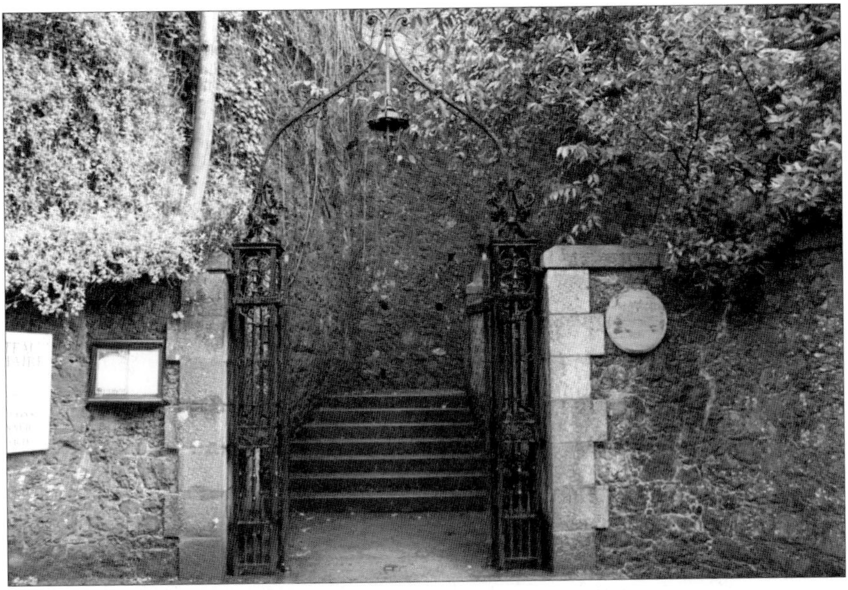

Fig 33 The gates from Graham & Banks that face the north side of the valley. La Chaire had electric lighting so the light that can be seen on the arch could be original.

Fletcher and Ethel returned to Jersey on 23rd March 1899, and as soon as they had booked into the Grand Hotel on St Helier seafront they set out for La Chaire. Fletcher was very pleased with the work of the builder, Springate, but he was extremely displeased with the work of his gardener, Sharman, who had been engaged before they had left Jersey on 1st January. His diary entry explains how he felt:

> 'The Winstanleys drove out with us to La Chaire. I should not have known the place. The veranda and tiled roof have altered the whole appearance. All Springate's work has been splendidly done. Sharman however has behaved shamefully. He has never watered the garden once since I left and has planted out the bamboos this weather and has made a mess of everything besides keeping the garden in a very untidy state. Have decided to dismiss him.'[87]

Sharman was duly dismissed the next day and Springate was asked if he could recommend someone to temporarily look after the garden. He recommended a gardener named Albert Smith and Fletcher interviewed him for the job on Saturday 25th March 1899. Springate lived in Gorey and so did Smith which is how the two men must have known each other. Fletcher makes reference to the fact that Smith was on a month's trial and that the gardener in overall charge was a man named Walter. Fletcher had not made reference to this man until now so it is unclear what his role at La Chaire was before this. On Saturday 1st April 1899, Fletcher and Ethel moved into La Chaire, they were both glad to get in as for some time they had been living in hotels.

Fletcher did one last thing before moving in and that was to inform two local businesses that for the first time in many years the garden of La Chaire was no longer open to the public: 'Wrote to Downs & Gregory's stables and to the Rozel Hotel saying that La Chaire gardens are in the future closed to the public.'[88] Since the death of Samuel Curtis in 1860 the garden had been open for public viewing and had in fact become part of a regular weekly visit by tourists who would arrive in the excursion car provided by Downs & Gregory's stables. The Rozel hotel was also used by tourists who wished to visit La Chaire and required refreshment. The garden had become very well-known and admired as 'The Rozel Tropical Gardens' and played an important part in the Jersey tourist trade in the nineteenth century.

There are many old photographs of the excursion cars as Jersey's tourism industry expanded in the second half of the nineteenth century and they became well subscribed. This service was the forerunner of the coach tour, which is still a popular tourist attraction in Jersey. The horse-drawn cars called at the main hotels for passengers between 10 and 11 am, then dropped them back around 5.30 pm. A seat on the car would cost around 2s 6d, which included the services of a tour guide who accompanied the passengers. As well as offering all the normal tourist information some guides would sing or play musical instruments.

At the summit of the garden on its eastern edge there is a water storage tank. Construction of a tank is not mentioned by Fletcher, nor is the installation of

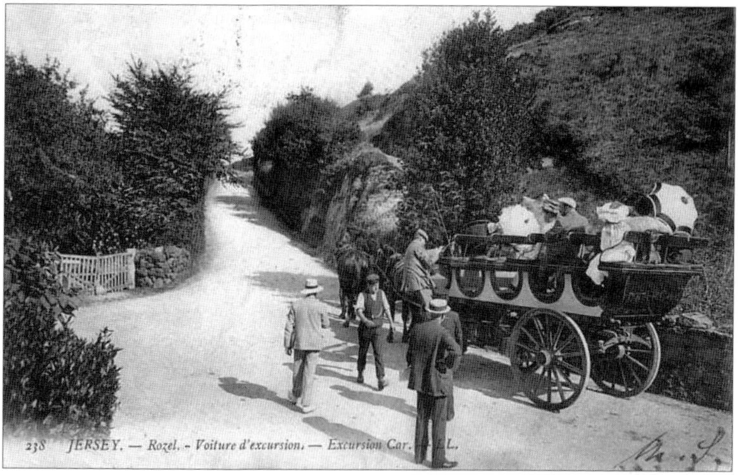

Fig 34 The postcard shows tourists re-embarking on the excursion car after having visited La Chaire. The photograph was taken towards the end of the nineteenth century sometime before March 1899.

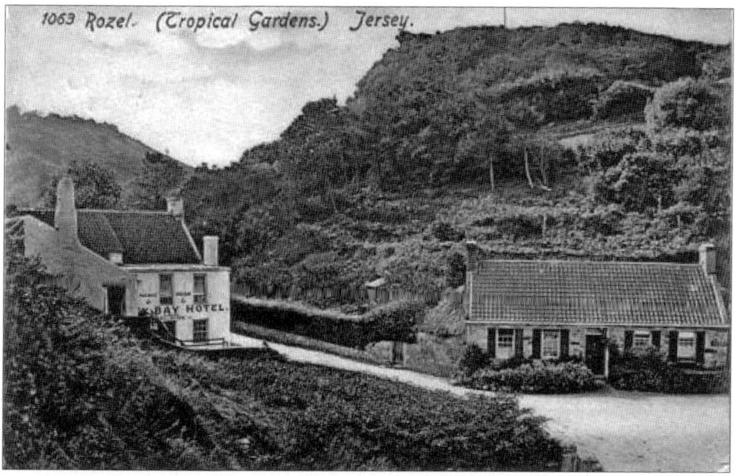

Fig 35 The Rozel hotel, where visitors to the garden of La Chaire would sometimes stay overnight or just take lunch, tea and dinner. This photograph was taken before the tenure of Fletcher at La Chaire. This is evident because the servant's house and the chateau itself are not visible. The hotel looks in the postcard much as it does today. To the right of the hotel, on the hill, is the garden of La Chaire.

the first pump that pushed water up to a head of around 200-250 feet. Unless Fletcher simply thought the tank and pump installation were not worthy of mention in his diaries, it must be assumed they were already in place. This is the most likely scenario as Fletcher would probably have discussed the installation of such important elements in the garden. Curtis would have constructed the tank for watering purposes but it is known that he never felt the need to install a full, piped irrigation system. Fletcher does state in a diary entry for 3rd April 1899 that he tried to run the pump but that it was out of order. If the pump was new and only just installed it would be unlikely to be found out of order so soon. Fletcher wrote: 'Tried to run engine but it was out of order. Sent for Harper's engineer.'[89]

Fletcher then proves that the pump and tank were already in position: 'Harper's engineer came out and thoroughly overhauled the engine. Ran it all day. Tank nearly full.'[90] The pump needing an overhaul meant it had been previously installed but not been used for a while and had lacked regular maintenance. It was powered by hot air which operated a hydraulic ram but it was not particularly reliable as diary entries discuss regular breakdowns with the engineer visiting on numerous occasions to repair it. In 1901 it was replaced with an electric version which was installed by a firm from England called Drake and Graham. This company were also fitting out the chateau with electric lighting. Fletcher wrote:

> 'Drake from Drake and Graham came over from England and he, Lloyd and myself arranged where to put all the lights. He also arranged to put an electric motor and pump instead of a hot air engine to pump the water to the upper rain water cistern.'[91]

The new pump was powered by batteries (accumulators) and a new engine house was constructed right by the stream which is still in place today. The cost of the new pump and building was high, and this with other costs concerned Fletcher. He noted his worries in a diary entry:

> 'The engine house and accumulating room will cost £300 to complete. This is an enormous sum. These extra expenses are mounting up dreadfully.'[92]

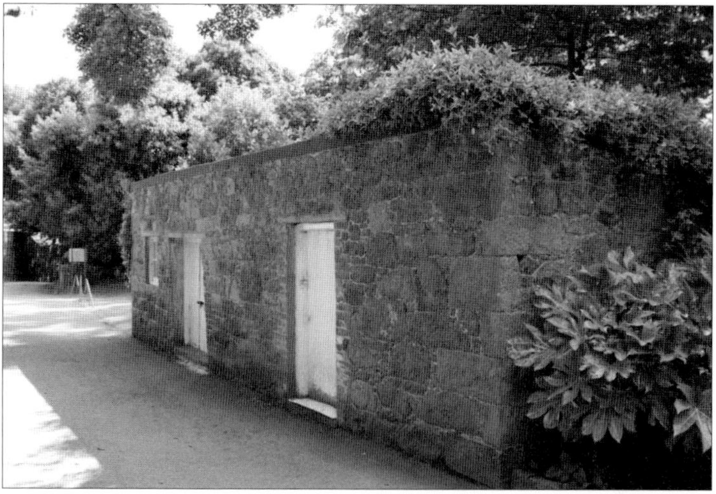

Fig 36 This photograph shows the engine house and accumulating room. The far end of this building still has the reservoir tank in the floor to hold the stream water that was then pumped 250ft up to the storage tank. The closest end was where the accumulators were kept. The engine house is still in excellent condition and is no longer in the ownership of Chateau La Chaire.

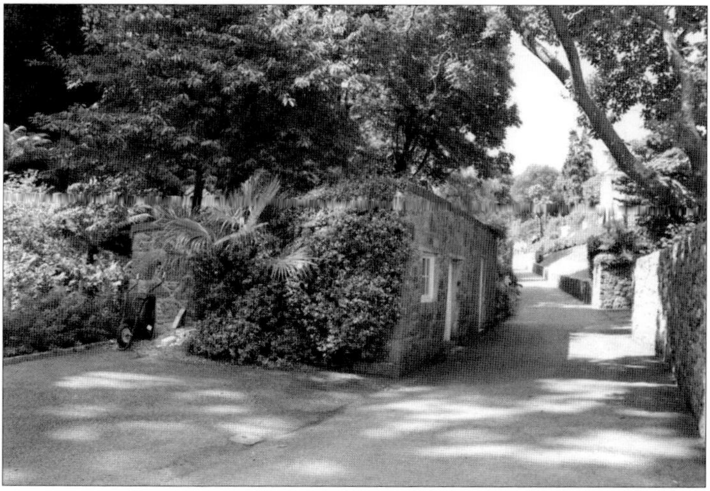

Fig 37 The engine house sits right on the edge of the stream and because of the size of the engine and accumulators it had to be a large building.

The pump drew water up from a deep tank which would have already been in place for the hot air version. Then the new engine house was built around it with an extra room being constructed for the batteries (accumulators) which provided the power. The water from the stream was diverted into the pump house through a sluice gate and into the tank when needed. The sluice was closed off when the pump was not being used and the tank was full. The original tank had to be repaired before the new arrangement could work. Fletcher wrote: 'They are getting on well with the new engine house and accumulating room. The leak in the tank has been patched.'[93]

The electricity to the house also came from the new accumulator room and was not without its teething problems as the fuses could often burn out. The engine house and accumulator room had been completed in early January 1902 and the final parts needed for the pump had arrived. The system worked more efficiently than Curtis's hot air system as described by Fletcher:

> 'The belting has arrived for the pump and Hopkins (Drake and Graham's Man) got it to work and pumped a lot of water into the tank. The little engine works well at a greater rate than before.'[94]

Now water was being pumped efficiently to the top irrigation tank, a series of pipes with taps at the ends were run from it, to positions all over the garden. Two of Fletcher's original taps can still be seen.

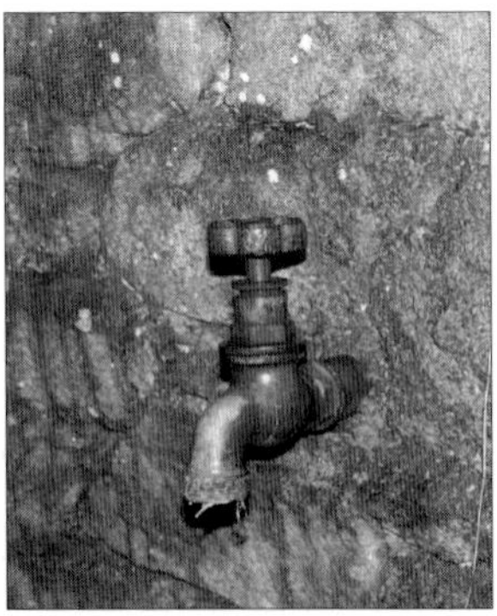

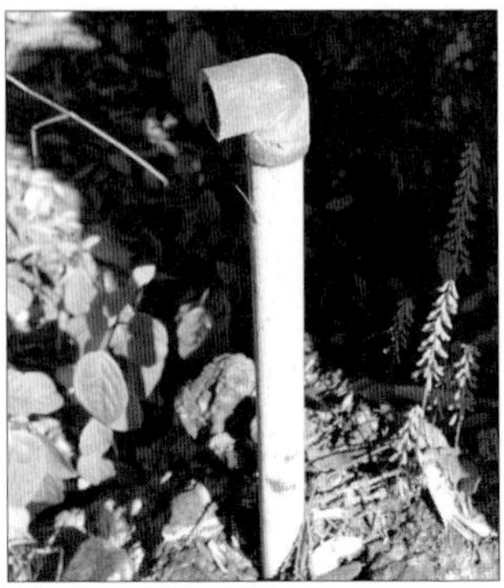

Left: Fig 38 One of the two surviving taps installed by Fletcher after the new pump had been installed. Right: Fig 39 Over the remaining garden the old irrigation pipes fed from the top storage tank can still be found. The end is threaded to take a tap.

The top irrigation tank at La Chaire sits at a head of 250 feet. This height would give a pressure of 86,600 pounds per square inch. The tank held 80 cubic metres of water, this figure calculated from its diameter and depth, which is 8 metres x 5 metres and 2 metres deep. The tank now has a depth of 1.5m but over one hundred years it would lose half a metre to sludge build-up without a lid, or 7.5 centimetres with a lid. There is no longer a lid on the tank, it was originally wooden and has long since rotted away. There is a 2.5 - 4 centimetre diameter outflow which was designed to give a consistent and controllable feed to the garden; however this could fluctuate and be difficult to regulate if the water level dropped, lowering the pressure.

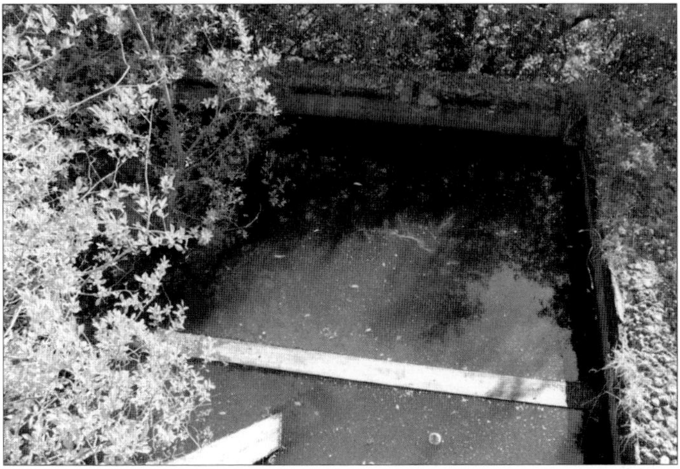

Fig 40 The top storage tank where water from the stream far below, was pumped up via the engine house

The tank also became the source of the feed for Fletcher's waterfall which at times seemed to be difficult to control. He wanted to keep the waterfall flowing at a slow but steady rate. It descended around 150-175 feet into the pond and fell directly from the pipe on the top storage tank. In the April of 1899 he describes his idea to keep it running: 'Lovely day, warmer. Started the waterfall very slightly on, and I intend to keep the water just dribbling in this way all the summer day and night.'[95]

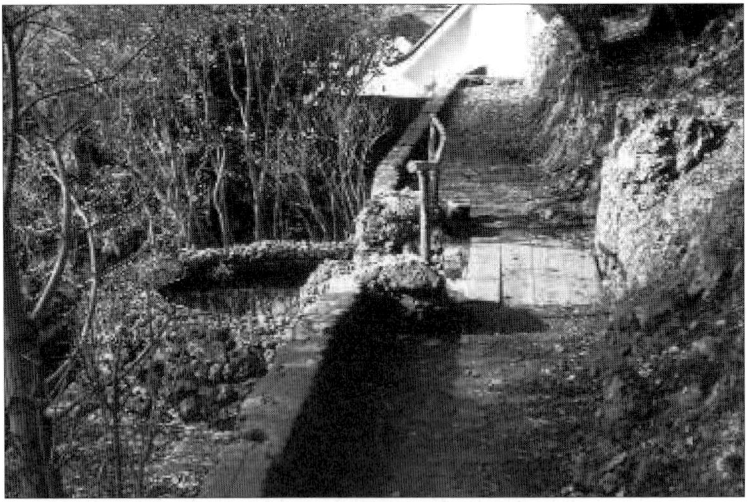

Fig 41 The pond as it looked in 2004. Fletcher's waterfall emptied into it.
The Rozel Conglomerate edging is still clearly seen.
Since 2004 the pond has become overgrown and derelict.

When Fletcher arrived at La Chaire the top irrigation tank was exposed. Curtis had not deemed it necessary to disguise it but Fletcher did not wish to see it and arranged to have it hidden behind rocks. By 1900 he was using another builder as well as Springate, a man named Lloyd. He made an entry relating to the tank and to Lloyd: 'Lloyd came out this aft and we arranged to put up the large boulders round the tank for £50.'[96]

By the second week in December the rocks had been taken up to the top of the garden. This must have been an extremely hard and labour-intensive task.

As previously stated, early in 1899 Fletcher had been in communication with the Surrey nursery firm, Gauntlett. By 5th April he wrote that he had sent them a cheque for plants that he had ordered. Then, on 9th April, the plants had arrived as he entered in his diary: 'Unpacked the bamboos and plants from Gauntlett which are mostly small plants.'[97] The significance of the Gauntlett order was not just its size but that the owner of the nursery and one of his men arrived in Jersey on 11th April to oversee and support Fletcher and his gardeners with the planting. Fletcher noted that: 'Gauntlett and his

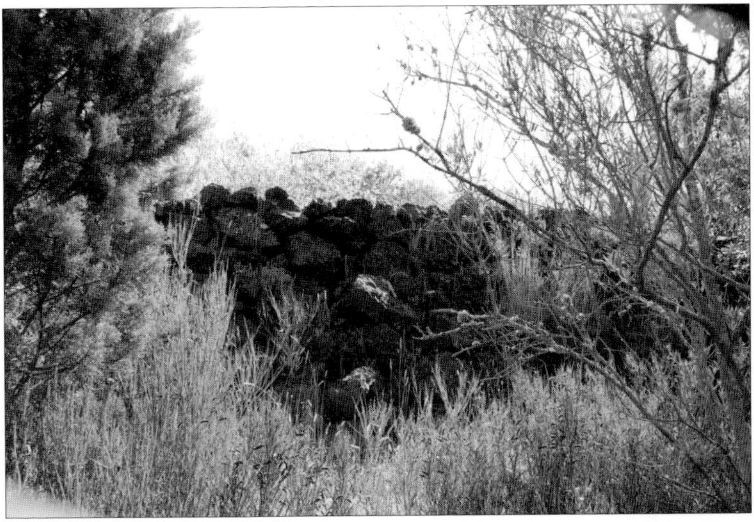

Fig 42 This photograph shows the rocks that Fletcher paid his builder £50 to fix in place around the tank with the intention of disguising it. Fletchers raised, round seating area is just to the left of the tank. The rocks hide the tank from this area.

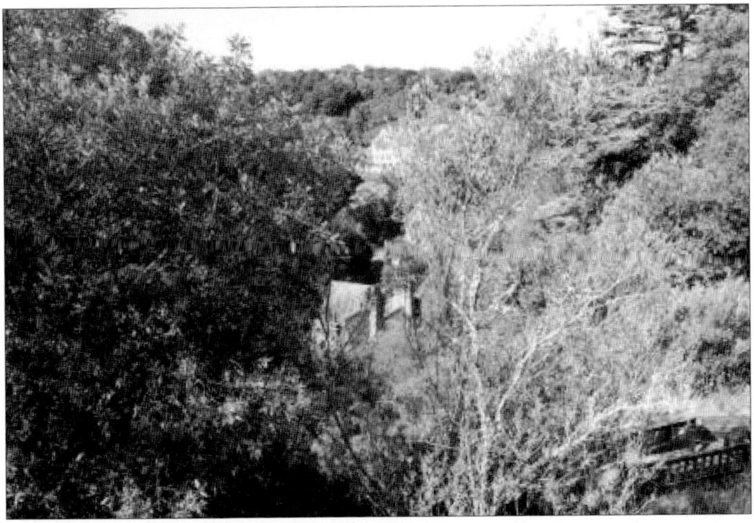

Fig 43 The view of La Chaire around a hundred feet below taken while standing on the rocks placed around the top water storage tank

man arrived. Went very carefully over the gardens with him. We start planting tomorrow.'[98]

The Gauntlett order was large and the price of the plants, coupled with paying the bill for Mr Gauntlett to come over to Jersey with an employee, constituted a considerable cost. Fletcher and his team also had to contend with the aftermath of Sharman, the gardener whom Fletcher had previously sacked. Fletcher notes the work now taking place and the input of Gauntlett and the impact of Sharman's neglect:

> 'Cold and windy. Planting begun. Planted six large Chamaerops fortune to form an avenue. Also planted out most of the bamboos. Gauntlett superintended the planting and we are making great efforts to get the place out of the state in which Sharman left it.'[99]

Fletcher describes the garden as being in a considerable state. It really does seem that Sharman totally neglected his duties while Fletcher had been away. There are numerous diary entries detailing the mess that the garden was in. Even so planting went ahead as planned. There were many bamboos being put in, some considerable amount of them as Fletcher alludes to in his diary:

> 'Cold and wet. Poured heavily nearly all day. Planting continued. Ordered a lot more bamboos etc. Intend to cover nearly all the pockets that remain unplanted with Bambusa palmata 'veitchii' and tessellate.'[100]

Planting proceeded until complete on 10th May. New plants arrived at regular intervals and Mr Gauntlett travelled to and from England to supervise. All the time Fletcher was on edge, worried that the work was not progressing as it should or that plants were not arriving on time. The neglect of Sharman was also still playing on his mind.

Fletcher gives an idea in his diary of the type of plants that were being ordered for the garden. He notes that on 15th April the 10 Falconeri bamboos arrived along with ivy-leafed geraniums and silver ivies. Bamboo was by far Fletcher's favourite plant; there were many different species planted all over the garden. He also gives a diary update on how his builder Springate is progressing with his side of the work in the garden:

'Replanted several crimson ramblers today. Began planting the silver ivies. There now remains to be done by Springates men in the gardens as follows:

- Completion of rustic rails staining and varnishing same-should take a fortnight.
- The 3 remaining walls on w. side-one is up should be finished next week.
- The gardeners steps down from reservoir.'[101]

On the last day of April 1899, Fletcher reports that all the roses had been planted and tied up on the iron arches and on 2nd May the majority of the plants sent by Gauntlett and the ones he had ordered from Ludwig Winter were in. The main bulk of planting had been completed although there was still a lot of work to do. Fletcher described what still needed to be done:

> Planting continued. Put in the tree ferns up the shady path and started planting the hybrid rhododendrons which will take some time. Gauntlett will not be done this week.[102]

Fletcher was concerned that even though the planting was progressing fairly well the building work in the garden was taking far too long. He made two diary entries over two days in early May. It can be seen that desperation was creeping into his writing. His depression did seem to make the situation worse than it probably was and it would appear he was unable to enjoy what he had, and what he was achieving in the garden.

His diaries painted a bleak picture of how he thought things were progressing:

> 'Matters seem to be getting worse instead of better. None of the bamboos and plants from Gauntlett turned up and so he is delayed here another day. The engine has gone wrong and neither Walker nor I are able to put it right. Have sent for Harper's man. I thoroughly watered all the dwarf bamboos this evening. The weather is lovely and it is a very great pity the work is not yet completed.'[103]

Then, over the next few days and following his despair, the pump had been repaired, Gauntlett had finished all the manuring and planting and

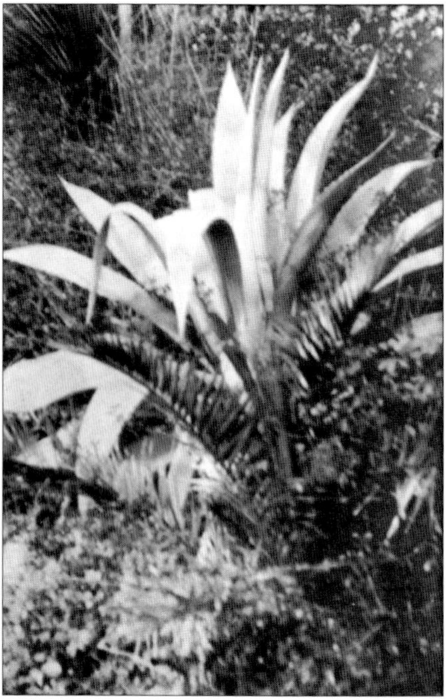

Fig 44 This photograph was taken by Charles Fletcher at La Chaire. The date is unknown but it shows one of his agave plantings.

the mess left by Sharman had been rectified. The first tranche of work Springate was undertaking also had an end in sight though Fletcher did note that it would be years before the garden and the bamboo in particular would make a decent show. All that remained for the time being was to settle his account with Gauntlett and Ludwig Winter. The bill from Gauntlett arrived five days after the planting, manuring, and labelling had been completed and came to £620. This was a considerable sum of money at that time.

For the next few months Fletcher noted in his diary the progress the new plants were making. He and his gardeners had to carry out a lot of watering at this early stage. He wrote that the bamboos were shooting well. Fletcher was always looking at making changes to the garden and discussing ways in which it could be improved. For example he would discuss with Smith his gardener different plants to try, as he mentions in his diary: 'Have decided to cover one of the new walks that we have to put up with Clematis and I wrote today for Jackman and Sons catalogue.'[104]

The gardeners were also heavily manuring the new beds. Manure had been used when planting but it seems a good layer was now being applied as mulch. This task took around two weeks with extra men employed to bring it up from the road and to spread it. In an entry he describes this task:

> 'Fine day very warm in the sun. Manure carting still going on. I had to engage two extra men today. This aft I spread manure over most of the top pockets containing palmata bamboo.[105]

Fletcher and Ethel would every so often travel to London to visit friends or conduct business. On one such trip in October 1899, Fletcher visited a nursery called Cutbush, at High Barnet, London. Cutbush's nursery no longer exists but it was once a considerable size and sold a wide and impressive range of plants. The nursery has now disappeared under what is the intersection of the A1 and M25. Fletcher details this visit and lists the plants that he saw and ordered for dispatch to La Chaire:

> 'We lunched at the Trocadero and went by train from Kingsy to High Barnet to go over Cutbush's nursery garden. Bought there for La Chaire, 3 golden oak trees, 2 variegated Sycomore, 2 dozen mop headed acacia, 1 silver poplar, one dozen lilac trees in variety, some hollies, two American oak, 2 purple beech, 12 ivies in pots, a weeping ash and two weeping willows etc etc….' [106]

In January 1900 Fletcher wrote to Cutbush and added more to this order as well as making some changes. He asked for laburnum, *Rhus cotinus*, and requested that the weeping trees be replaced with tulip trees. On 16th February, Fletcher wrote to the Cutbush nursery to inform them that they were now ready to receive the plants. The Cutbush trees arrived on 2nd March and were unwrapped. But according to his diary they were not in the best of condition. Either they suffered from a long hard journey, which was most likely, or Cutbush sent inferior stock, which was unlikely. Fletcher wrote: 'Cutbush's trees arrived much broken and seem a poor lot.'[107] Sadly not one of these plants has survived the passage of time.

In October, 1899, a new phase of construction and planting was undertaken. There seems to be a lack of planning ahead as some of the palms received from Ludwig Winter had to be lifted to widen the palm walk. There are no original garden plans or maps in existence and only a few photographs that Fletcher took so it is impossible now to guess where the palm walk may have been.

For the new work Springate was asked to provide quarrymen to blast away tons of rock to make new garden terraces and planting pockets. There are still today around 94 planting pockets on four main terraces. The quarrying work to shape the new garden started on 18th October 1899 but did not finish until 16th February 1900. Masons were working behind the quarrymen, constructing the new planting pockets and terrace walls. Behind them came the carpenters who were attaching rustic trellis to the walls that had already been completed or were of original Curtis construction. Apart from the trellis, the work that these men completed still stands today and forms the structure of the garden. Fletcher does not state how many men were working at La Chaire during this busy period but it must have exceeded twenty, as the garden was a hive of activity. Once the terraces had been blasted out and the new walls constructed it was then the turn of Fletcher's gardeners to fill the pockets with soil ready for planting, as described here:

> 'The masons began on the small walls. The gardeners will have finished preparing the top rose garden this week. Putting trellis on the old walls nearly finished.'[108]

The new top rose garden was to be planted with roses ordered from the firm Cant. Fletcher ordered these on 6th November and all 138 of them had arrived and were planted by 30th November.

The work to fill the many pockets was a hard and slow job, requiring a lot of soil. Fletcher had an advert published in the local newspaper asking if anyone had topsoil for sale. In general he was pleased with the progress of the quarrymen, masons and carpenters but he thought the filling of the pockets needed to be speeded up. He wrote:

> '...the masons getting on with walls but am afraid that filling up with earth will be very slow work. Have decided to engage 5 other men on Monday.'[109]

As well as taking on the extra labour to fill the pockets, a lift was engineered to transport the soil to them, remembering that from the road to the top of the garden was a steep climb of approximately 250 feet. Fletcher describes this work:

> 'We are now hard at work filling up the terraces with soil, a very long job but we have rigged up a truck on wheels which works on rails and is drawn by a winch.'[110]

It took a few days to perfect this invention but when it was working correctly it transported a lot of soil very quickly. The invention was so successful that it meant the gardeners were waiting for the masons to complete before they could fill up the pockets and terracing. Fletcher gives the impression again that the work was going along well, but the new garden must have looked like a building site:

> 'The men all at work on the winch and truck filling pockets. Masons at work on walls and carpenters putting in pegs for trellis. The rustic pergola is being pushed on in Springate's shop at Gory.'[111]

During this period of intense construction Fletcher was communicating with nurseries and ordering plants and seeds. At the end of January he wrote to Veitch to order Japanese cherries and flowering peaches. He also wrote to Suttons for seeds. There are also constant references to the progress of filling up the terraces and planting pockets with soil. The whole construction process was slowed down at times as January 1900 saw very poor weather. There were bitterly cold winds, snow and hard frosts. The weather was still awful in March but the Springate pergola was completed and erected on site with Cant's climbing roses planted against it. Smith the gardener was planting bamboo and dwarf roses while men were still hauling soil up the steep valley side to fill the few remaining empty pockets. But by early March Fletcher was able to write: 'We finished with the trolley and winch today and had them taken away. We shall resume planting next week.'[112]

The first phase of the alterations and improvements had been reached: the soil that had been lifted and piled at the top of the new garden was transferred into the few pockets that needed it and final planting and transplanting of plants that had to be moved for the quarrymen was taking place. The hardest part was the transplanting of some large bamboos as Fletcher described:

> 'We transplanted with great difficulty owing to their size and weight the Nobilis bamboos and other large ones. Continued planting the other plants, cherries, roses etc.'[113]

The final stage of the first phase was to tidy up the garden, complete more planting and lay gravel underneath the pergola and on the terrace around the

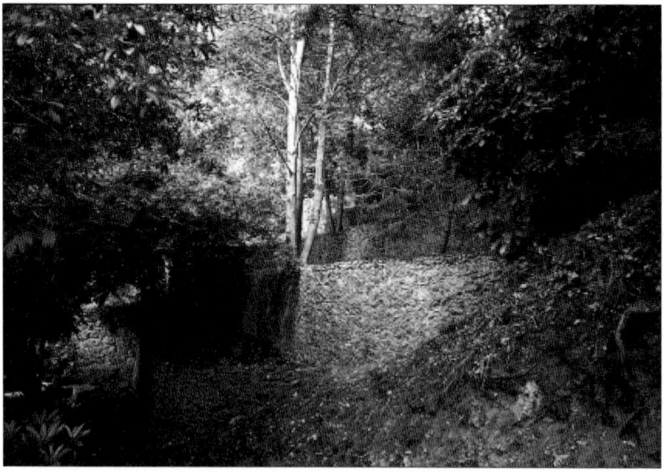

Fig 45 This is the only part of the garden that has long stone terraces so this must be the new part of the garden that Fletcher discusses. The terraces start below the ones seen here and finish at the top of this end of the garden. This new part marks the second phase of the gardens construction and would fit the description as to the location of the new garden. Magnolia Cottage which was built below this terracing was named after this part of the garden.

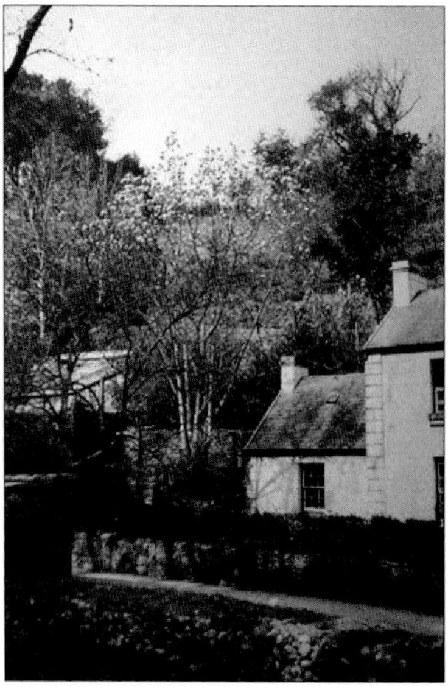

Fig 46 This photograph shows Magnolia Cottage. Just to the left of the lower section of the building can be seen the *Magnolia Campbellii* that was planted by Harriet Fothergill shortly after the death of her father Samuel Curtis. This plant and other magnolia were instrumental in Fletcher's planting magnolia in this area This area was also the second phase and last section of the garden to be completed.

house. The Chamaerops palms were also replanted in front of the chateau on the terrace. Fletcher was still constantly buying new plants, some from Becker's Nursery in Jersey. From them he purchased double-flowered nectarines, arum lilies and conifers. He does note that on 9th April, Mrs Phebe Rooke paid a visit to La Chaire. Her reaction to the changes at her old house is not considered worthy of note in the diary but they must have surprised her immensely. The change from what she had known was considerable. Fletcher describes her visit:

> 'Fine but rather dull, rain this evening.
> Mrs Rooke called this afternoon and went over the garden.
> Everything in the garden is very backward owning to the absence of sun and warm weather. Nothing is making a start except the bamboo tessellate and veitchii which are throwing up shoots.'[114]

Fletcher was pleased to note in June that the bamboos were making good growth as were all the other plants, this continued to be noted in his diary for the rest of the summer. The growth of the roses pleased him but that would have been helped by the regular feeds they were having of Clay's Liquid Manure.

In the August he wrote that Baal had become the head gardener. He did not state if this was a different Baal to the builder who was business partner to Springate or the same man and there is not a clue regarding this in the diary; 'Rain for a short time this morn but not enough to do any good. Baal started as head gardener here today.'[115] Fletcher does not say why Smith left his employ and Baal took over; no reference to any animosity between gardener and employer was mentioned.

~ 8 ~
The work continues

In August 1900, Fletcher commissioned a new architect named Lloyd to design further alterations to the chateau. This involved digging into the cliff face, so the chateau could be extended towards it. He also writes about creating a new garden but makes no firm reference in that year's diary to where this was to be. It is not difficult now to work out the exact location. He talks of long terraces of stone to keep up the soil so this has to be in the part of the garden that is on the far left side of the chateau as you look at it, as these stone terraces are long and are some distance from the main body of the garden where the first phase of construction and planting had taken place. The other factor is that the new garden is in the area of another property built since the time of Fletcher, called Magnolia Cottage. In the garden of Magnolia Cottage are Magnolias purchased and planted by Fletcher as well as a *Eucryphia cordifolia*. Fletcher writes in his diary that this was to be an area of the garden where Magnolias were going to grow. He wrote: 'Am going to make the new garden in long terraces of stone to keep up the soil and shall make a speciality of Magnolias.'[116] This evidence gives conclusive proof of the location for the new garden at La Chaire.

Before work had got underway on the house alterations and the last phase of the garden's design, Fletcher had an important visitor, A. M. Andre, the French landscape gardener. He describes the visit in his diary:

> 'A. M. André came out this aft and went over the garden. He appeared very pleased with them and invited me to see his garden at Cannes next winter. He took the names of several bamboos, roses etc. He is one of the celebrated family of André's the botanists. The clematis Madame Edouard André was named after his mother and his father discovered *Genisto andreana*.[117]

The general maintenance of the garden carried on and Fletcher was ordering more plants. He made orders with Veitch, Cant and Kelways. From Kelways the order for three dozen delphiniums was made to replace hollyhocks and dwarf sunflowers that had failed in the summer. From Cant he ordered two dozen of the rose Paul's royal scarlet. Veitch were to supply three dozen of an unspecified violet species. He also made orders for other plants as he describes in his diary:

> 'Fine and sunny but cold NE wind which of course we did not feel here. This morning we planted the delphiniums from Kelway. There were 3 dozen (2 dozen collection C and I dozen collection D) and two included gratis. Price of the three dozen £ 7-2-0. I found that we just succeeded in planting the three terraces below the pergola with these and I wrote to Kelway for three dozen more (2 dozen collection D
>
> 1 dozen collection E. Price £ 11.8.0. I also wrote to Veitch for some plants of Eremus. I know nothing about these beyond what I have read but they appear to be handsome plants.'[118]

Fletcher also ordered some peonies from Kelways for the new terrace garden with the idea of making a peony walk. Planting then took place when all the plants had arrived.

Gardeners under the new head gardener, Baal, were instructed to lay a deep mulch of manure over the whole garden. Baal arranged the supply of this and Fletcher commented on its good quality. To manure the whole garden took around five days to complete. Before the work commenced on the new garden the last tasks the gardeners undertook was to transplant and plant some roses as described by Fletcher:

> 'We transplanted two of the best yellow roses on the veranda and put them on the pergola and we also put the Rosa ards rover in between. This should be effective.'[119]

Now the scene was set for the chateau alterations to start and the new garden to be constructed. The work on the new garden started on Tuesday 20th November 1900 and had been completed by the end of February, 1901.

The work on the new garden was completed much faster than the first phase as the area was far smaller. Springate would have assumed that his firm would be undertaking the new works but Fletcher decided against this. There appears in the diaries a slow but steady dislike and distrust of Springate although Fletcher never criticised the quality of the work he was undertaking. The new builder, a man named Green, was commissioned instead, although Springate was still working at La Chaire and building servants' cottages in the village for Fletcher. This may also have been the reason for employing Green; Springate may have been hard pushed to start other work and of course it is unlikely that the impatient Fletcher would want to wait. Fletcher wrote about the new arrangements:

> 'We arranged that Green should move the greenhouse, not Springate, also the summerhouse to the terrace. We also arranged with him to build the walls and pockets for the new gardens and the 12ft shelter wall on the very top.[120]

Fletcher unsurprisingly did not take long to find fault with Green and his men, which must have pleased Springate greatly. That is if Springate was even aware of his employer's displeasure as Fletcher displayed in his diary:

> 'Green's gang really do not appear to have done much and I don't think he has enough men on the job.
>
> The walls in the new part have not progressed much and they have put no boulders in position yet around the tank.'[121]

Fletcher was writing his diaries from the Grand Hotel St Helier, now that work had started on the chateau extension and alterations. In the same diary entry as above Fletcher writes: 'The blasting behind the dining room has shaken one of its walls and had damaged one or two of the garden walls but it cannot be helped.'[122]

Although work had already started on the chateau and the new garden the final cost had still not been estimated by Lloyd. Fletcher was still visiting Lloyd in his St Helier office on 18th December although blasting behind La Chaire had been going since early November. Had the cost had been prohibitive once work had begun, as it could very well have been, it would have been a risky project for Fletcher. On Friday 21st December, 1900, Fletcher and Ethel had left the Grand Hotel and were on their way to the South of France. En route Fletcher called to see Lloyd to hear the estimate for the work on the chateau improvement. The estimate was purely for the chateau and not the garden. He recalled this meeting in his diary:

> '…Gave Green an advance of £160 for work done at La Chaire.
> On way now, called at Lloyd's office. He told me his estimate for the alterations and additions to the house worked out at under £6,000 which is satisfactory. The old greenhouse is being erected on its new site. Baal, Walker and two men are hard at it filling the walls in the new garden.'[123]

While over-wintering in the South of France, Fletcher communicated almost on a daily basis to Lloyd and Baal. He constantly enquired regarding the progress of the new garden and was pushing for its completion. He also wrote to Kelways and Veitch to order plants. Fletcher in the entry below asks Baal for a full report on the garden and he also wrote to Veitch with an idea he had regarding planting the new garden:

> 'Sent Baal a cheque for his wages also Walton's and Hamon's and told him to write to me fully how the work has progressed.
>
> Wrote to Veitch to ask them if they would undertake the planting of the new garden. Told them I would spend £100 in plants for it.'[124]

After a few worrying reports that had concerned Fletcher the answer to this letter was very positive and in fact Baal was ready to start planting. He also said that the *Prunus pissardii* and the Persian peach were already in bloom. Baal did not know that Veitch might be undertaking the planting. It is possible that Fletcher did not fully trust Baal. He had acknowledged that he was very keen and wanted to please but there was reluctance on Fletcher's part to fully trust his judgement, as can be seen from this entry:

> 'Got letter from Veitch about planting the new garden at La Chaire. They want to send a landscape gardener and probably make an expensive job of it. Decided therefore to get Baal to plant the garden. Wrote Baal to that

effect and also to Veitch telling them to send plants ordered last August and I also ordered others such as *Cydonis japonica*, ceonothus and jasmine to cover the walls. I gave Baal very clear directions as to how to plant and I think he will manage it all right. Shall write to Kelway and order tree peonies from him.'[125]

Unfortunately history has not recorded Baal's reaction as a head gardener to being given explicit instructions on how to plant. Obviously Fletcher did not consider his initial instruction on how to plant enough and was worrying over his decision to allow Baal to plant the new garden. On 5th March he wrote another long letter with more instruction and this time also included a rough plan of where he wished all the plants to go. Baal was also writing and sending at least one letter a week to keep Fletcher up to date with progress. Baal was proactive in suggesting ideas for the garden and Fletcher did agree with virtually all of them. In one letter this can be seen:

'Got letter from Baal explaining the progress of work at La Chaire and asking about putting roses on the walls alongside the paths in the new garden. For this I ordered 20 Marichal niel roses from Cant of Colchester today. Baal also sends plan of suggestions for piece of ground below greenhouse.'[126]

Fletcher did order the tree peonies, three dozen of them from Kelway for a cost of £13..4..0. He also wrote to Veitch and informed them that they would only be required to supply the plants and not send anyone to the Island to undertake the planting. Over the next few weeks Fletcher ordered from Veitch many magnolias, a variety of Japanese shrubs, azaleas, new species of rhododendrons, almond trees, sweet pea seeds, and metal plant labels. Altogether there were over a hundred rhododendrons and over fifty azaleas ordered from Veitch. More plants were requested from Kelway which included herbaceous peonies, more delphiniums, asters, gallardias, *Physalis franchetti,* and three dozen single pyrethriums. The Kelway order came to £48..00.

In early April Baal wrote to Fletcher and included three photographs of the new garden. He did not seem overly excited by what he saw:

'This morning 3 photographs of the new garden at La Chaire which Baal had taken arrived. Am afraid the walls will take a long time to cover. At present it looks more like the ruins of a Roman amphitheatre than anything else.'[127]

Fletcher returned from France and at the end of April had booked himself and Ethel back into the Grand Hotel, St Helier. In his diary he reiterated the point he made regarding the stark walls while viewing the photographs he had received from Baal:

'We drove out to La Chaire today. The new gardens will I am sure be splendid in time but at present of course the new walls are very unsightly. Some magnolias are out and…a very fine one.'[128]

Overall he was pleased with the garden and how Baal had conducted himself during his absence. Twice over a three-day period he wrote in his diary how well the garden was progressing and that in a few years it would be a lovely place. He did agree with Baal that extra labour would be required over the summer if they were to keep on top of the work. Fletcher also commented on the progress of the new roses: 'Paul's carmine pillar rose is beginning to flower. There should be a fine show of roses this year.'[129]

Fletcher's mood did fluctuate considerably. During May, while work was still going on in the chateau, they resided in one of his cottages in Rozel harbour that had just been completed. The reason for moving out of the Grand Hotel was purely economic. On 8th May, his diary entry is positive, apart from a moan over the pump breaking down again:

'We are beginning to get things shipshape here at last. Some of Veitch's azaleas are coming out and are fine plants. There are rose buds everywhere and bamboo shoots by the hundred. I am gradually being repaid for all the trouble and expense.'[130]

But then six days later, Lloyd, by an oversight, had darkened his mood considerably and he wrote:

'Lloyd had not sent Merryweathers man out about the engine. This is an infernal place to live in. All are thieves. Held forth on this

> subject rather freely in the club. Shall get disliked for it no doubt but that is immaterial.'[131]

The reason for this outburst and obvious indiscretion in the club would have been down to a bout of depression or more likely his alcohol intake or even a dangerous combination of the two. Even though his mood was black on 15th May he still ordered 100 clematis plants from Veitch to cover the trellis on the new walls.

Fletcher was keen to note all the new plants and watch their progress. Of all the hundreds that had gone in over the past year only a few had failed. He notes that he had lost some of the delphiniums and the species of bamboo, *hindsii*. This had flowered, causing it to die. When he was ready to replant the bamboo planting pockets he found that his old gardener, Sharman, had filled up the pockets they were planted in with rubbish instead of loam. He then had to have all of it removed and replaced with soil. This made him extremely angry and he began to question if this problem would be discovered elsewhere in the garden.

He commented in late May how good the garden was looking even though he was very concerned over the lack of recent rain. There was an exceptionally dry period until July, as he commented on:

> 'The gardens are looking very well indeed. The gardens had to be watered all over again today. This E. wind dries everything and rain is badly wanted.'[132]
>
> Some of the ramble roses are out such as the yellow aflaia, the pink euphrosyne. Thalia is just starting. *Reine olga de wurtenburg* is in flower on the pergola so is ards rover. Paul's carmine pillar is a beautiful site on the walls. One of the most striking trees in the garden is I think Paul's royal scarlet. The bamboos are throwing up any number of shots and should double their size this year. One mitis has enormous shots just beginning. The delphiniums have picked up and the poppies at the cross look lovely.'[133]

Despite the drought, plants were still being ordered even though the gardeners could not keep up with the need to water. Fletcher noted that some of the plants were even shedding leaves to reduce transpiration. In mid-June he ordered pots of *Rosa wichuriana* from Veitch to cover the new garden walls. Fletcher disliked the bare walls and wrote that he wanted them covered at any cost. Later in the year he ordered 50 Rosa wichuriana along with 6 *Clematis Montana*, and some *Wisteria multijuya*. The plan for the clematis was to grow them up through certain trees in the garden.

The year 1901 ended with another project in the planning and then final construction stage. Fletcher wanted to enlarge the front terrace, which inevitably meant the lifting of plants that had not been in very long. Again there was not an overall chronological plan set out right at the start of all the construction work. This meant an amount of unnecessary work being carried out with its respective cost and time delay implication.

Lloyd had suggested commissioning Pulham and Son to make a new entrance to the house and to redesign the terrace, but they never undertook the work. No reason is given in the diaries as to why this was the case. In a diary entry Fletcher wrote: 'Lloyd is writing to Pulham and Son about making an artificial rock entrance with small waterfall.'[134]

Fletcher described some of the plants that would have to be moved to accommodate the new terrace and a suggested carriage drive right up to the front door:

> 'Moved some of the bamboos and dracaenas to make room for the enlargement of the terrace in front of the house and the new entrance. We put these plants in the new pockets at the end of the dining room and made a very effective group. Also planted a conifer and a small Irish yew in the top pockets by the boulders.'[135]

The New Year of 1902 came and saw Fletcher worried about the amount of money he had borrowed from the bank. He had up to 12th January spent £13,010 on the chateau and garden. He was also worried about being conscripted into the Jersey Militia at this time due to the Boar War. Fletcher even spoke to Ethel about just using La Chaire for the odd holiday and moving to Malta to avoid being called up. London was considered too dangerous and not a suitable place to live at that time as smallpox was rife.

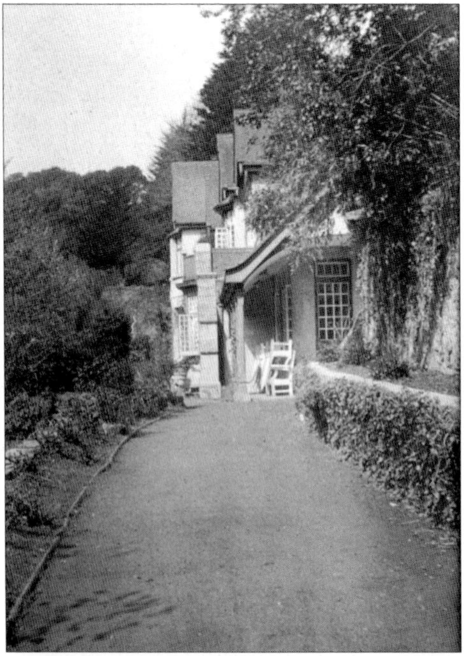

Fig 47 Charles Fletcher took this photograph of the terrace sometime before it was extended and widened

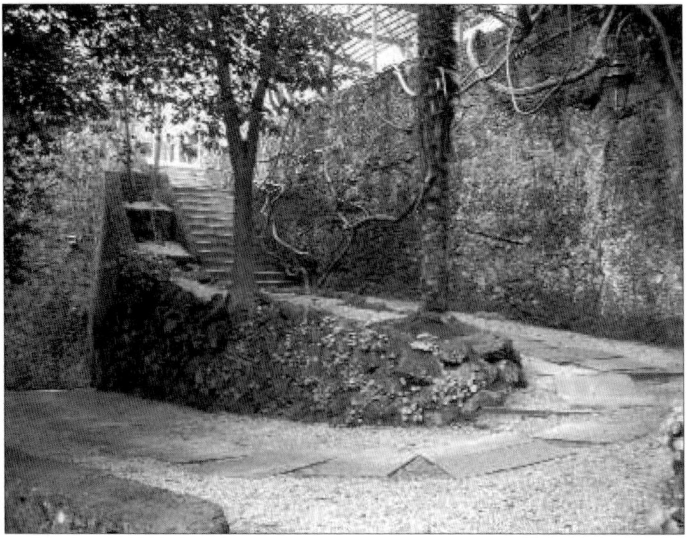

Fig 48 Fletcher's new entrance that still looks as it did when initially constructed

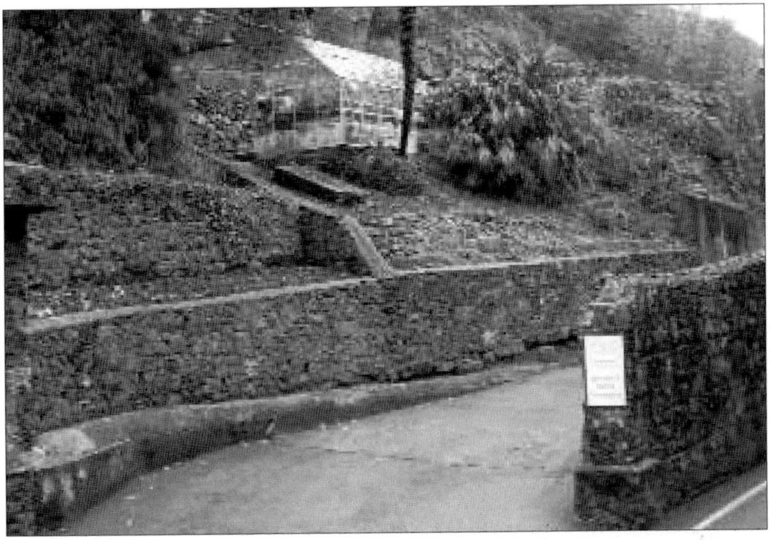

Fig 49 This photograph is of the far end of the drive and shows the terrace walls that were completed in the second phase of the gardens design. The carriage drive enabled horse drawn and motorised vehicles to stop right at the front of the chateau. The lane at the end is narrow so Fletcher had a turning cycle built opposite.

Now that the garden had been completed there was room for the first time to grow vegetables. A variety of vegetable seeds were ordered from Suttons as Fletcher explained:

> 'I wrote to Suttons for vegetable and flower seed today. For the first time we have room in the gardens to grow vegetables.'[136]

Then by March, Fletcher was making diary entries regarding the very mild spring and commenting on how well forward all the plants were. He was still moving plants to better positions and buying some to cover the new terrace railings at the front of the chateau as well as covering up the chateau walls. He detailed the plants and work carried out:

> 'Wrote to Cant for 14 Ayrshire roses to plant on the terrace railing in front of the house. Today we planted 5 bignonias, *Grandiflora radicans* and *Radicans sanguinea* to grow up the house.

Planted 4 scarlet trumpet honeysuckles in the new garden. This cold E. wind could not be felt in the garden. *Bambusa palmate* has started to throw up shoots.'[137]

The shelter belt originally planted by Curtis was obviously doing its intended job as Fletcher makes numerous comments on the cold and at times high winds. The garden as Curtis envisaged was very well protected. This can also be ascertained by the plants which all seem to be thriving and avoiding severe weather damage. The plants were also supported by generous feeding of liquid manure which went on for some months. Fletcher commented on how rough the north-east coast could get:

'It blew practically a gale all day which however could not be felt in the gardens. Nearly all the climbing roses are in bud and we ought to have a great display this year. Some of the Japanese cherries should be in flower in a few days if we get decent weather.'[138]

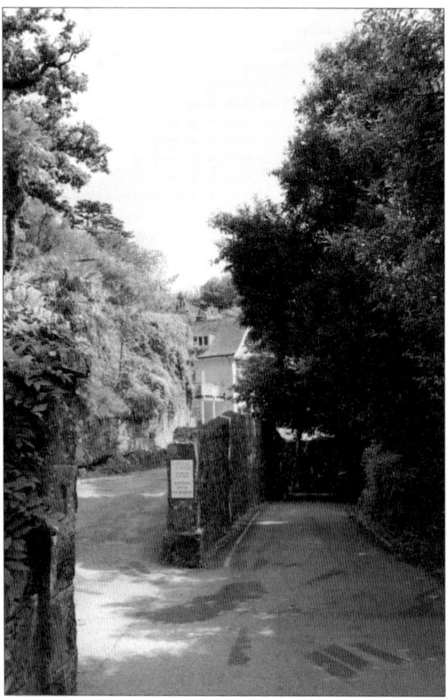

Fig 50 Photograph taken looking back at the chateau from the end of the drive and demonstrates the access now available

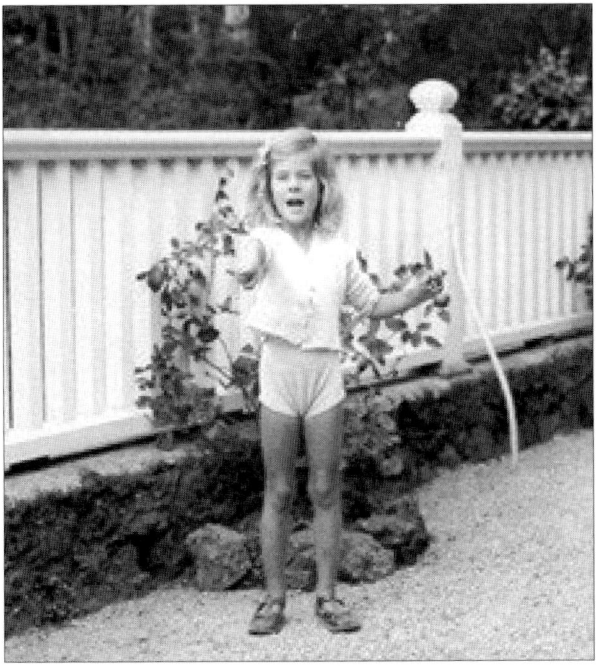

Fig 51 This photograph was taken during the 1930s, before the German Occupation of Jersey. It clearly shows the railings that had been put in place by Charles Fletcher. The girl in the photograph is the daughter of Mr and Mrs A. Nicolle who bought La Chaire in 1932.

The new entrance was completed by the end of April and an iron electric lamp that is still in place was attached to provide light in what is a dark area. The gardeners also planted out cannas, ivy-leafed geraniums, a *Phoenix canariensis* and two small *Chamaerops fortunei* around the entrance. The last of the many trellis panels were also being fitted and painted green all over the garden. Even today the old post holes can still be seen. The loan from the bank had reached £14,990 but by the end of November the bank had advanced the sum of £22,000, but as already stated his securities were performing poorly. But at least he knew that now the major work had all been completed.

During the restoration attempt in 2003 the round stone area next to the water storage tank surrounded by the boulders was cited as being a gun emplacement, built early in the nineteenth century. This round area does not have a slope in or out of it and access to bring a large gun up to this part of the garden is extremely limited if not impossible. There is a gun platform lower down near the harbour and the hard standing for this is large and reinforced. The size and construction of the area at La Chaire would make a gun emplacement impossible. Fletcher in his diary for 18th June 1902 makes compelling evidence that this area always has been a simple garden feature:

> 'Am going to level a round platform on the very top of La Chaire where we can put seats and get the view. The view over the sea looks lovely today.'[139]

The entries regarding the garden grow sparse until 1903 but there are still comments on how it looked and how it was performing. Fletcher also wrote that they moved back into the now completed chateau in July, and everything was finished. Unfortunately he was starting to feel the effects of chronic liver disease and he was clearly depressed. This is easy to ascertain from his diary entries at that time. Much to Ethel's considerable annoyance he bought a car; this occupies much of his time but he may have enjoyed the diversion from the worry of the endless construction and the garden.

Fletcher and Ethel were in the south of France at the start of 1903. He was worried about the bad weather reports he was receiving from Jersey. The weather was extremely cold with frost and snow. In his diary's first entry for 1903 he writes that he was anxious about the plants at La Chaire. Not until the start of April did Fletcher mention anything of any consequence again about the garden. By this time he had returned from over-wintering in France and had obviously purchased some plants from the Nabonnand nursery in Golfe-Juan, the Alpes Maritime. Its founder, Gilbert Nabonnand, died in 1903; Fletcher probably dealt with his son Paul.

The nursery specialised in China and Tea roses and produced over two hundred varieties. Fletcher though did not purchase any roses from them but some more exotic plants. He recorded what he purchased: 'The plants from Nabonnand Golfe-Juan arrived and we planted the camellias, yuccas and one or two sabal palms.'[140]

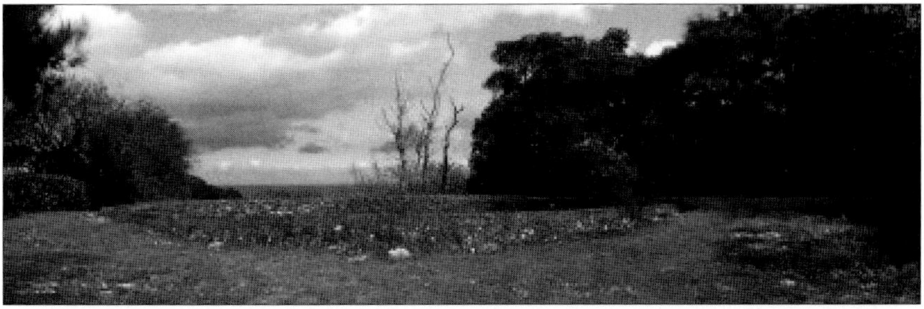

Fig 52 During the failed restoration attempt this round stone built area was thought to be a Napoleonic gun emplacement. This area has no main access for a gun of the size needed to protect this part of Jersey from French invasion. It would also be far too small to be built for an artillery piece. As the diary entry states, this is the highest point of the garden and so the place for a seating area. There would have been a circular wooden deck on top of the wall. This area commands wonderful views of the sea and of France.

On 22nd April Fletcher wrote to Veitch and ordered 37 more Wichuriana roses. He had already planted at least fifty of these in 1901 and would go on to order more in 1906 in two batches, although those came from Paul and Cant. The idea with these roses was to cover as much of the terrace walls as possible. The roses and all of the plants that came from mainland England or France were picked up by his cart at the harbour in St Helier. Fletcher described the planting and the use of the Wichuriana roses:

> 'We planted the Wichuriana roses 37 in all. Some we put in the old garden but most in the new and on the terrace to hang down the wall. These roses I think will make a great difference to the gardens and in time I hope not a vestige of the walls will be seen either in summer or winter. I also had three small larch trees planted by the boulders at the top of the hill. The aspect of these should be good.'[141]

Fletcher could not stop buying plants to fill the garden. In May 1903 he wrote to Veitch again and requested two plants of *Embothrium coccineum* and from Becker's nursery on Jersey he purchased two *Kentia* palms, two *Dracaena* and two *Yucca varigata*. Not all the plants performed as well as he would have hoped – the Marechal niel roses in early April were suffering from canker;

Fletcher could not find a cure for this disease but records trying:

> 'This afternoon I had all the herbaceous peonies and also the delphiniums staked. Our Marechal niel roses are suffering from canker. I don't know what to do for this and in all my books cannot find anything like a proper remedy.'[142]

The canker did not seem to spoil these roses too much as in early May they were picking baskets of them from the terrace walls for vases inside the chateau.

Apart from a few entries regarding the problem with greenfly and replacing some almond trees with bamboo, as well as hosting a visit from the Jersey Gardeners Society, no other entries were recorded concerning the garden in 1903. The Society visit may or may not for some reason have been expected as there seems an element of surprise in the recording of it from his diary: 'We lunched at the Grand. Drove back here where we found nearly 100 of the Jersey Gardeners Society going round the garden.'[143] Fletcher was extremely proud of the garden and it would be out of character to not take the opportunity to show it off to visitors.

As previously stated, no diaries exist for 1904 and 1905. The last year that Fletcher recorded was for 1906 but the entries finished in early July. The last

Opposite page, Fig 53 The illustration displays the positions of the key features of the garden at La Chaire and provides some orientation for them, and the planting discussed in the text. Behind and to the right of Magnolia Cottage was Fletchers 'new' garden, the Magnolia garden. Also the wide terrace built by Fletcher can be seen as well as the long carriage drive with its turning half circle, opposite. The whole area behind the chateau was terraced by Fletcher and contains the first part of the garden to the right and the Magnolia garden to the left, what Fletcher called his new garden. Fletcher planted a large number of Magnolias in the area behind what is now the garden of Magnolia Cottage. The rest of the garden was full of roses on trellis and filled with the hundreds of plants he purchased. It is unclear now where all the plants were placed as the diary entries are vague and written as though the reader knows exactly how the garden looked, as Fletcher obviously did. This means he was not very descriptive when discussing planting positions. There are no planting plans that survive.

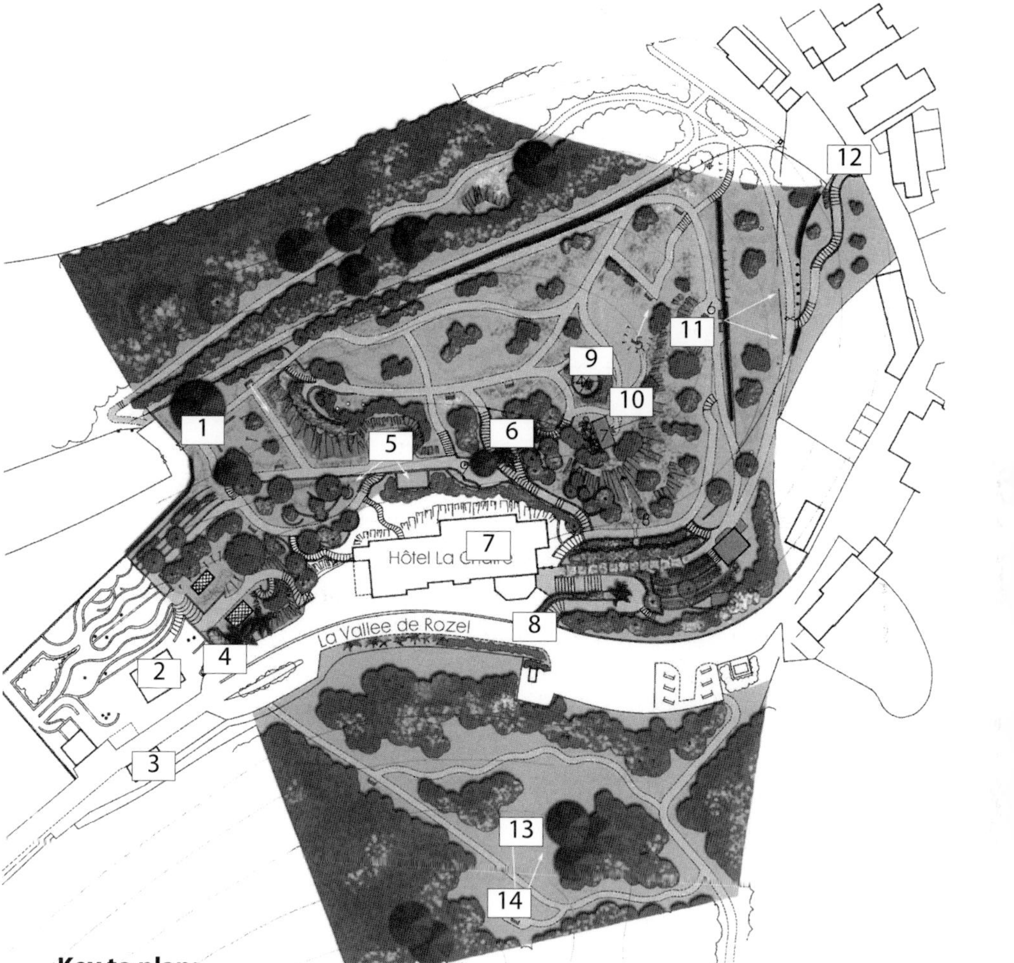

Key to plan:

1 Monterey cypress
2 Magnolia Cottage and the site of Fletcher's 'new' garden
3 Fletchers pump house
4 Fletchers carriage drive
5 Site of Curtis summerhouse
6 P*hoenix canariensis*
7 The Chateau
8 Entrance
9 Fletcher's round seating area
10 Reservoir and boulder screen
11 Site of the Cross
12 Rozel entrance
13 Site of Curtis Himalayan glade
14 View point overlooking valley

The area to the left of the cross was the part of the garden first planted by Fletcher few months record basic maintenance being carried out, such as liquid manure being applied. More roses were purchased to cover various arches and a pergola. By the time the entries stopped, La Chaire had well over two hundred roses of all types planted in the garden. Fletcher had made a rose garden near the top with arches and so removed the rustic railings that were there. He described this:

> 'We put up two rose arches at the top rose garden. Cleared away the rustic railing and the ramblers on it near the paulownia. Most of the afternoon was spent watering the new garden.'[144]

For these arches he purchased the roses, Mrs O. G. Orpen, Le Vesuve, Debutante, and Mrs Flight.

Fletcher also asked Baal to find a third man for the garden as he wrote that every day there seemed more and more to do.

The diaries finish with his very last entry on Saturday, 14th July: 'This afternoon planted nearly all the wichuriana roses.'[145]

It is very sad, given the vast amount of money Fletcher lavished on La Chaire and the extreme pressure to which the whole project subjected him, that he only benefited from and enjoyed it for such a very short time. In fact the garden was still undergoing small alterations to finish it completely when he died. Neither Fletcher nor Ethel were rewarded by seeing the garden totally completed. What happened to it in the period after his death in 1907 is not known. However it does seem that towards the end the animosity between Fletcher and Old Walton had played itself out. There are two simple but telling entries that Fletcher made about Walton: 'The Waltons came round and went over the gardens. Gave him some palmata bamboos.'[146] A week later he wrote: 'We stayed here all day. Walton showed me his flowers. He has got some good ones.'[147]

In 1921 Fletcher's son sold up to Mr Edward Roberts and the garden of La Chaire started a slow and gentle decline.

Conclusion

When Fletcher's son, Charles Hugh Fletcher sold La Chaire in 1921 the property left the family for good. No surviving family member has ever visited the chateau since, although it is the hope of Sarah Cursham, Fletcher's granddaughter, that she will be able to do so. Charles Hugh Fletcher sold La Chaire to Edward Roberts and no details survive of what Roberts did in the gardens. From Fletcher's diaries it can be assumed that by 1921 the garden must have been fully mature. Most likely Roberts would only have needed to carry out and continue routine maintenance to keep the garden under control. But it is also possible that Fletcher's son, who did not reside in Jersey, did not employ a gardener, and until 1921 it may have become wild and overgrown. Roberts sold La Chaire to Mr and Mrs Arthur Nicolle in 1932. Mrs Nicolle was a very keen gardener and corresponded with Kew regarding La Chaire. Charles Raffill, head of the Temperate House at Kew, visited La Chaire in April 1933 at the behest of Mrs Nicolle to advise her on the redesign of the garden.

Mr and Mrs Nicolle moved back to England just before the German occupation of the Channel Islands as Mr Nicolle had come out of retirement to manage a large manufacturing company. When the German army occupied Jersey, troops and officers were billeted in various houses around the Island. It is not recorded whether German troops lived at La Chaire but it is known that a Frenchman, born in Guernsey by the name of Yves Marie Le Bloas, was the sole gardener and had been left in charge of the property.

One factor in the decline of La Chaire, but one that has not been resarched fully, was the German acquisition of plants from the garden. A German officer ordered the digging up and root balling of a large amount of plants that had been planted by Fletcher and subsequently by Mrs Nicolle. It has been said locally that these plants were destined for a botanical garden in Germany, possibly Berlin.[148] Albert Le Bloas, the gardener's son, remembers being with his father while he was lifting the plants and his father transporting them down to Fletcher's pump and battery house, using a cart. He remembers well his father telling him not to touch the plants and to keep at a safe distance, as he watered the root balls with battery acid. Le Bloas was not going to allow the plants to survive for the enjoyment of the Germans. Almost certainly the plants were not destined for Germany but for an officer's commandeered house on the west side of the island. There are no records of the amount of plants that were lost but the son of Mr and Mrs Nicolle, writing a brief account of La Chaire in the 1960s, is able to state a few of the plant names:

> 'There was nobody in charge except for one gardener. Much to his disgust some of the best magnolias, a *campellii* grown by Mrs Nicolle from seed, and a *grandiflora Goliath*, to name only two, were carefully packed with enormous balls of earth round their roots.'[149]

After the war in 1947, the Nicolles sold La Chaire and the property then went through a succession of owners. Land that had been part of Fletcher's garden was sold off and the estate is now far smaller than when Fletcher died in 1906. This also makes it difficult to ascertain where Fletcher had certain elements of his estate positioned.

During the early part of the last decade an attempt was made to restore the garden. This costly attempt failed, leading to financial disaster for the main organiser. There was also a tremendous amount of animosity for the restoration plan and some also directed at the organisers. The fight against the restoration became bitter and personal. It was partly centred on the fact that the infrastructure in Rozel could not cope with the proposed visitor numbers. Car parking would have been a major issue, not to mention the local people who could see their peaceful way of life being ruined.

The present book has been an attempt to relate the history of La Chaire in an accurate and chronological way. A report commissioned by the restoration team in 2003, written by Philip White, the Director of Hestercombe, presenting ideas on the future of La Chaire is in places inaccurate. For example, he does not even refer to Charles Fletcher and attributes the entire garden infrastructure to Samuel Curtis. He also makes incorrect assumptions on Curtis's character by writing in the report that, 'Curtis was a religious zealot who would preach

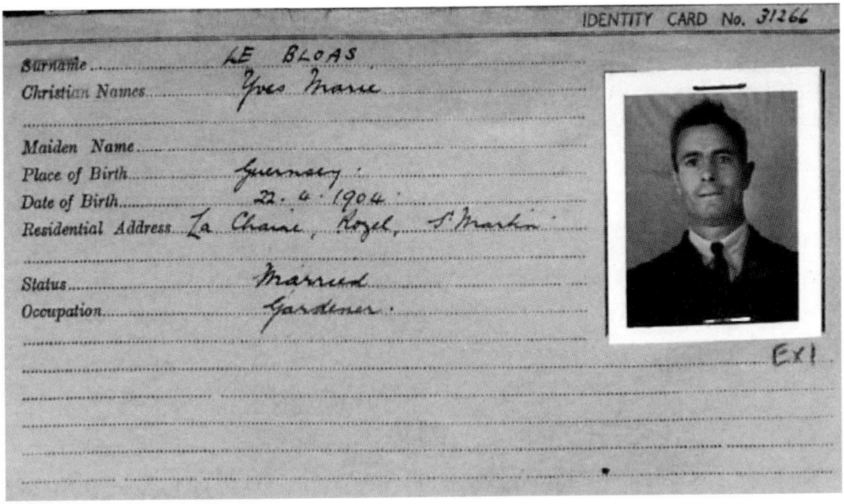

IDENTITY CARD No. 31266

Surname LE BLOAS
Christian Names Yves Marie
Maiden Name
Place of Birth Guernsey.
Date of Birth 22.4.1904.
Residential Address La Chaire, Rozel, St Martin.
Status Married
Occupation Gardener.
Ex1

Fig 54: The Identity Card of the head gardener at La Chaire
during the years of the German Occupation

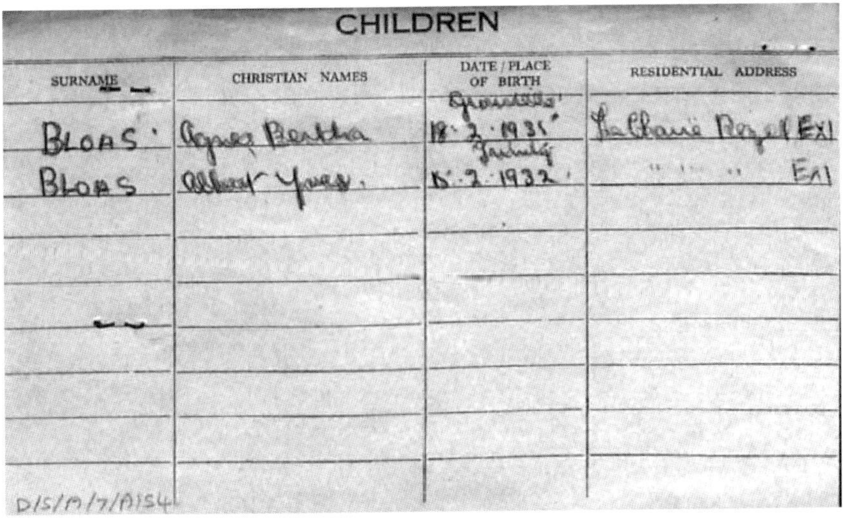

CHILDREN

SURNAME	CHRISTIAN NAMES	DATE / PLACE OF BIRTH	RESIDENTIAL ADDRESS
Bloas.	Agnes Bertha	Grouville 18.3.1931.	La Chaire Rozel Ex1
Bloas	Albert Yves.	Trinity 15.2.1932.	" " " Ex1

D/S/A/7/A154

Fig 55: This illustration shows the identity card of Le Bloas, proving that he lived in the gardener's cottage at La Chaire with his wife and two children during the Occupation. Albert, the son, at the time of writing, in March 2014 is still alive and well and living in Jersey.

to the gardeners while they worked in the garden.'[150] This account has shown Curtis to be a Quaker and, though religious, he was certainly not a zealot – Quakers simply do not preach.

The focus of articles on La Chaire and the backbone of the proposed restoration were centred on its ownership by Curtis. This is to the detriment of Fletcher and all the major infrastructural changes he made to La Chaire. Curtis did create the garden but by 1898 most of his plants had been lost with few exceptions. The restoration plan aimed to put La Chaire back to the time of Curtis, but from Fletcher's diary entries it can be seen clearly that once Fletcher had completed his work the garden bore very little resemblance to the original Curtis creation. All the changes made by Fletcher proves that the restoration with an emphasis on Curtis would have been fundamentally flawed.

Fletcher did nothing remarkable in his life apart from having the vision to create a garden of outstanding beauty and interest. His role at La Chaire has been totally overlooked, and his part in the construction and planting has been glossed over to give prominence to Curtis who was considered an important plantsman. It was felt by the restoration team that the name Curtis was capable of attracting people to visit the garden as he was part of the Curtis family who produced and owned the *Botanical Magazine*. Samuel Curtis was indeed important in terms of his horticultural skill and knowledge. The events in his life that led to the creation of the garden at La Chaire are documented as is the vital role played by Fletcher. The garden may now be seen primarily as Fletcher's garden and his role should no longer been seen as of lesser importance than Curtis.

From the weather data collected and the letters written by Curtis, it is clear that the garden of La Chaire was not the protected environment in which to grow sub-tropical and tropical plants for any protracted period of time. Curtis was incorrect in thinking that La Chaire could support the plants he wished to grow. The garden was exposed to and suffered from severe cold snaps that, by the end of the nineteenth century decimated it, destroying most of the plants grown by Curtis. Mean winter temperatures in Jersey are higher than those on the mainland but bitterly cold weather can cause devastation.

Tim Smit (from Heligan and the Eden project) while in Jersey was influenced by the marketing carried out by the restoration team and made his sweeping statement that he thought La Chaire could be Eden with the roof down. The planting by Curtis concentrated on non-hardy plants and was an experimental plantsman's garden rather than being a garden for purely aesthetic reasons. His plants were at the mercy of even small temperature fluctuations and suffered accordingly. Fletcher grew plants that were hardy and would not have looked out of place on the mainland. This meant that the garden was not so much at the mercy of a winter cold spell and also that Fletcher's planting is perhaps of less interest in the history of La Chaire.

La Chaire is now almost derelict with no hope at all in the foreseeable future of undergoing essential restoration. If Fletcher's builders had not been so professional the garden infrastructure would have been lost by now. Virtually all the planting from any period has gone and the garden is overgrown with weeds and self-seeded trees. The Hatton Hotel Group which owns La Chaire have full occupancy for almost every day of the year so do not see the necessity in spending money restoring the garden. This is shortsighted as visitors would most likely increase revenue. The hotel does not even employ a full-time gardener to keep the garden from at least getting any worse.

Resistance to any new restoration plan would be robust and vigorous but economic conditions in Jersey would probably not be favourable. Jersey has undergone public spending cuts like the United Kingdom. The last attempt resulted in failure so it is unlikely that anyone would wish to end up in the same position. The only way that La Chaire could be restored would be for the hotel to sell the property and for it to be acquired by an extremely rich individual with funds enough to return it to a private garden.

Fundamentally there is a case to be made for La Chaire to return to its former glory. The garden is an important part of Jersey's heritage and does have historical, botanical and cultural significance for the island. Together with Sir John Le Couteur's garden at Belle Vue, La Chaire was a plantsman's garden and the plants grown were rare and important. Curtis was attempting to push the boundaries of what could be grown successfully in the island. There are still some plants of national importance in the garden that will be lost if not managed very soon. Some of those grown at La Chaire were used in *Curtis's Botanical Magazine* colour plates. Curtis received the early introductions into the United Kingdom of Bhutan rhododendrons and other new plants. Once he had received them some were sent out to other parts of Jersey and the mainland making La Chaire an important garden connected with plant exchange and movement. A restoration of the garden could lead in turn to the restoration of the once historic plant collection. At the very least this account will have recorded some of these plants for a future restoration project. La Chaire is important for what it once was and, if totally lost, Jersey will have let go a vital and important link with its horticultural heritage and its link with past nursery industries.

In the last few years there has been talk in Jersey of creating a new botanical garden in partnership with The Royal Botanical Garden, Kew. Such a garden and much like La Chaire would serve to attract visitors to the island which, since the advent of cheap foreign holidays, has suffered a sharp decline in tourism. La Chaire, in conjunction with complementary attractions, could increase revenue from tourism significantly and provide local employment for young people in the island, which is limited at present. The garden would also offer educational possibilities. The main college in Jersey, Highlands College, no longer offers full-time further education in horticulture. La Chaire could work in conjunction with Highlands and offer an apprenticeship scheme to reinvigorate interest in this subject and fill positions in the industry with local people.

La Chaire will continue to degrade. It will eventually become too dangerous to ascend the terraces. My hope is that the present book will be a permanent record of this once botanically and historically great and important garden, part of the original aim. I hope that one day La Chaire will receive the restoration it deserves and all the time, effort and money expended by Fletcher will not have been in vain.

Appendix 1: Bibliography

Primary

Curtis, Samuel: *The Glazenwood Horticultural Grounds of Samuel Curtis, FLS. 1831.* (Publisher not stated)

Curtis, Samuel: An address to the public, more particularly to those of the nobility and gentry who patronise horticulture; also, to the immediate patrons, friends and visitors of Glazenwood, new Coggeshall in the County of Essex. 1831 (Publisher not stated)

Curtis's Botanical Magazine, vol 54 (vol 1 of the New Series). 1827

Curtis's Botanical Magazine, vol 67, 1841

Curtis's Botanical Magazine, vol 68, 1842

Curtis's Botanical Magazine, vol, 69, 1843

The Cottage Gardener, xxiii, 1860

Diaries of Charles Fletcher 1898-1906. (Originals held by Mrs Sarah Cursham, the granddaughter of Charles Fletcher)

Jersey Archive D/Y/A/30/49 Will of Samuel Curtis, 1853

Jersey Agricultural and Horticultural Society, Annual Report(s) 1853, 1855, 1859, 1860. (Hand written reports)

Linnaean Society Proceedings xxii-xxiii, 1855-61 (Hand written)

La Chaire Gardens, Rozel Jersey. Historic Landscape Survey and Restoration Plan. Nicholas Pearson Associates. May 2003

Nicolle, A.V. A note about La Chaire. June 2, 1968 (Hand written note)

Royal Jersey Agricultural and Horticultural Society, Obituary written by the Honourable Secretary Frederick Browning, 1860

Royal Botanic Gardens, Kew Archives, Goods in 1848, 1858, 1888, 1892

Royal Botanic Gardens, Kew Archives, Directors Correspondence 33 fol..99 37 fol.86

Shepard, H.G. *The first hundred years of the Jersey Agricultural and Horticultural Society. (1883-1933)*

The Royal Society of Arts. Transactions of the Society. Manufactures, and Commerce, Vol 26. 1808 pp 1-20

The Illustrated London News, July 1, 1843, p.12 (Article and writer unnamed)

The Jersey Gardener: A Monthly Journal of Rural Economy for the Channel Islands

Secondary

Burleigh, A. B.: 'Samuel Curtis, FLS, 1779-1860'. *Journal of the Royal Horticultural Society*, pp. 324-328, 1933.

Desmond, Ray: *A Celebration of Flowers.* Collingridge Books. 1987

Hobhouse, Penelope: *The Story of Gardening.* Dorling Kindersley, London. 2002

Hyman, A., *The Gaiety Years.* Cassell 1975

Jean, John, *Jersey Horses from the Past.* Seaflower Books 2000

Lever, Colin: *La Chaire: Beyond the Garden Gate.* (ELSP 2011)

Nichols, R. A. H. & Hill, A. E., *Jersey Geology Trail.* Wentworth Press. 2004

Penny, David: *More Hidden Gardens.* London: Octopus Publishing Group, 2004

Russell, Tony: 'Jersey Cream'. *The Garden.* pp. 302-305. April 2004

Russell, Tony: La Chaire Garden. The Garden. *Journal of the Royal Horticultural Society.* April 2004

Stevens, Joan: *Victorian Voices.* Société Jersiaise 1969

Turner, Tom: *Garden History Philosophy and Design 2000BC-2000AD.* Spon Press Oxford. 2004

Vassallo, Domenico, *Jardins des Alpes.* Leonardo International, Milan 2006

Went, D. & Andrews, M.: 'Post-Cadomian erosion, deposition and basin development in the Channel Islands and northern Brittany, in the Cadomian Orogeny'. Geology Society. Special publication. No. 51, p. 293-304

Appendix 2: Interviews

Brewster, John: Former owner of La Chaire. Interview on the history of La Chaire.

Blake, David: Librarian, Quaker Library. Interview on the theory of Quaker Truth or honesty.

Bloas, Albert: Son of the former head gardener throughout the war years. Interview on La Chaire between 1939-1945

Cursham, Sarah: (Granddaughter of Charles Fletcher. Interview on the life of Charles Fletcher and his time at La Chaire.

Labey, Bruce: Dip. Hort. Kew M.L.A. M.I.Hort. Interview given on the failed restoration of La Chaire.

Petkovic, Angie: Interview on the history and failed restoration of La Chaire.

Sutherland, Rozelle (Société Jersiaise). Interview on the history of Jersey and La Chaire.

Appendix 3: Illustration references

Figure 1: Stephen Harmer, La Chaire, December 2012.

Figure 2: *id.*, La Chaire, December 2012.

Figure 3: *id.*, La Chaire, February 2014.

Figure 4: *id.*, La Chaire, July 2013.

Figure 5: States of Jersey Planning and Environment Department. 1:2500 Map

Figure 6: La Chaire Gardens, Rozel Jersey. Historic Landscape Survey and Restoration Plan. Nicholas Pearson Associates (May 2003).

Figure 7: La Chaire Gardens, Rozel Jersey. Historic Landscape Survey and Restoration Plan. Nicholas Pearson Associates (May 2003).

Figure 8: Harmer, La Chaire, July 2013.

Figure 9: Ordnance Survey, Southampton. Institute of Geological Sciences. Channel Islands Sheet 2. 1:25000 Series.

Figure 10: Harmer, Royal Botanical Garden Kew, April 2013.

Figure 11: op. cit.

Figure 12: op. cit.

Figure 13: op. cit.

Figure 14: Harmer, La Chaire, July 2013.

Figure 15: id., Royal Botanical Garden Kew, April 2013.

Figure 16: La Chaire Gardens, Rozel Jersey. Historic Landscape Survey and Restoration Plan. Nicholas Pearson Associates (May 2003).

Figure 17: op. cit..

Figure 18: Harmer, La Chaire, July 2013.

Figure 19: Photograph courtesy of Mr John Brewster, Rozel, Jersey.

Figure 20: Harmer, La Chaire, July 2013.

Figure 21: La Chaire Gardens, Rozel Jersey. Historic Landscape Survey and Restoration Plan. Nicholas Pearson Associates (May 2003).

Figure 22: Harmer, La Chaire, July 2013.

Figure 23: Harmer, Magnolia Cottage, Rozel. December 2012

Figure 24: Courtesy of Mrs Angie Petkovic

Figure 25: Courtesy of Mrs Sarah Cursham

Figure 26: *op. cit.*

Figure 27: Unknown provenance

Figure 28: La Chaire Gardens, Rozel Jersey. Historic Landscape Survey and Restoration Plan. Nicholas Pearson Associates (May 2003)

Figure 29: Harmer, La Chaire, December 2013

Figure 30: Courtesy of Roger Jones, Seaflower Books

Figure 31: Harmer, La Chaire, July 2013

Figure 32: *op. cit.*

Figure 33: *op. cit.*

Figure 34: By permission of David Le Maistre L.L. Postcard number 238

Figure 35: Courtesy of Roger Jones, Seaflower Books

Figure 36: Harmer, La Chaire, July 2013

Figure 37: *op. cit.*

Figure 40: *ibid.*, La Chaire, December 2012

Figure 41: La Chaire Gardens, Rozel Jersey. Historic Landscape Survey and Restoration Plan. Nicholas Pearson Associates (May 2003)

Figure 42: Harmer, La Chaire, December 2013

Figure 43: *id.*, La Chaire, July 2013

Figure 44: Courtesy of Mrs Sarah Cursham

Figure 45: La Chaire Gardens, Rozel Jersey. Historic Landscape Survey and Restoration Plan. Nicholas Pearson Associates (May 2003)

Figure 46: *ibid.*

Figure 47: Courtesy of Mrs Sarah Cursham

Figure 48: Harmer, La Chaire, February 2014

Figure 49: *op. cit.*

Figure 50: *op. cit.*

Figure 51: La Chaire Gardens, Rozel Jersey. Historic Landscape Survey and Restoration Plan. Nicholas Pearson Associates (May 2003).

Figure 52: *op. cit.*

Figure 53: *op. cit.*

Figure 54: Jersey Archive. Ref D/5/A/7/A154

Figure 55: *op. cit.*

Appendix 4: Research material

La Chaire Gardens, Rozel Jersey. Historic Landscape Survey and Restoration Plan. Nicholas Pearson Associates. May 2003

The Jersey Gardener. A Monthly Journal of Rural Economy for the Channel Islands

References

1 The elected Government of Jersey headed by the Bailiff

2 La Chaire Garden Restoration Plan APT.832. Nicholas Pearson Associates Ltd. May 2003. Appendix 4

3 Lever, Colin: *La Chaire: Beyond the Garden Gate*. Seaflower Books (2011)

4 A. B. Burleigh. Samuel Curtis FLS (Fellow of the Linnaean Society) 1779-1860. *Journal of the Royal Horticultural Society*. p. 327. 1933

5 Jim Gould. *The Journal of The Garden History Society*. Volume 19:2 Autumn. pp. 155-162. 1992

6 Jim Gould. *The Journal of The Garden History Society*. Volume 19:2 Autumn. pp. 155-162.1992

7 The theory of Quaker truth or honesty was given by David Blake, Librarian, Quaker Library, London in a phone interview on 23 July 2013

8 Twentieth Annual Report of the Royal Jersey Agricultural and Horticultural Society for 1853. Published in 1854

9 Royal Jersey Agricultural and Horticultural Society, Annual Report, 1855

10 Royal Jersey Agricultural and Horticultural Society, Obituary written by the Honourable Secretary Frederick Browning, 1860

11 Gould, Jim: *The Journal of the Garden History Society*. Volume 19:2 Autumn. pp 155-162. 1992

12 Kew Archives: DC (33) – English Letters (1853) f.99

13 Kew Archives: DC (37) – English Letters (1853) f.86

14 Gould, Jim: *The Journal of The Garden History Society*. Volume 19:2 Autumn. pp 161-162

15 Royal Botanic Garden, Kew Library Archives, Sir William Hooker letters items 437 and 439

16 Burleigh, A. B.: Samuel Curtis FLS 1779-1860. *Journal of the Royal Horticultural Society*. p.327. 1933

17 Historic Landscape Survey and Restoration Plan. Nicholas Pearson Associates Ltd. May 2003

18 Transactions of the Society volume 26 pp123-126

19 Burleigh, A.B.: Samuel Curtis FLS 1779-1860. *Journal of the Royal Horticultural Society*. p.326. 1933

20 Samuel Curtis. An address to the public, more particularly to those of the nobility and

Glazenwood, new Coggeshall in the County of Essex, 1831

21 Curtis, Samuel: *The Glazenwood Horticultural Grounds of Samuel Curtis, FLS*, 1831

22 *The Illustrated London News*. July 1, 1843. p 12. Appendix 2

23 Russell, Tony: Horticultural Director, La Chaire Garden. The Garden. *Journal of the Royal Horticultural Society*. P304. April 2004

24 Ordnance Survey, Southampton. Institute of Geological Sciences. Channel Islands Sheet 2. 1:25000 Series

25 The name reflects the colour of the rock.

26 A small chain of disputed Islands with Jersey sovereignty which lay approximately six miles off the north-east coast of Jersey. France disputes ownership.

27 While visiting Jersey in 2004, Tim Smit, fresh from the success of the Eden Project, was shown La Chaire to garner support for the intended restoration. He inadvisably called La Chaire 'Eden with the top down'- a statement that was more hopeful than factual.

28 David, Penny: *More Hidden Gardens*. Cassell Illustrated. London. pp.104-105. 2004

29 Hobhouse, Penelope: *The Story of Gardening*. Dorling Kindersley, London. p.254. 2002

30 Turner, Tom: *Garden History Philosophy and Design 2000BC-2000AD*. Spon Press Oxford. P245. 2004.

31 Hobhouse, Penelope: *op.cit*. P254. 2002

32 *op.cit*.

33 Desmond, Ray: *A Celebration of Flowers*. Collingridge Books. p.121. 1987

34 Chapter 1- 1.1 pp12/13

35 Hobhouse, Penelope: *op.cit*. p.252. 2002

36 Stevens, Joan: *Victorian Voices. An introduction to the papers of Sir John Le Couteur, Q.A.D.C., F.R.S.* La Société Jersiaise. Jersey. p. 244, 1969

37 Hobhouse, Penelope: *op.cit*.

38 Hobhouse, Penelope: *op.cit*. p.243. 1969

39 Historic Landscape Survey and Restoration

Plan. Nicholas Pearson Associates Ltd. May 2003

40 Tony Russell was the Head Forester of Westonbirt Arboretum from 1989 to 2002. He has appeared on various TV programmes and then become the Horticultural Director of La Chaire during the failed restoration. The quote was taken from a press release entitled The Samuel Curtis Garden, La Chaire, dated January 2003

41 Plants grown at La Chaire, 1850-1906. Historic Landscape Survey and Restoration Plan. Nicholas Pearson Associates Ltd. May 2003

42 Royal Jersey Agricultural and Horticultural Society, *Annual Report*, 1855

43 In 1818 *Thea viridis* was renamed as *Camellia sinensis*

44 Curtis, W. H. *Life of William Curtis, 1746-99*, 1941

45 The quote was taken from a press release entitled The Samuel Curtis Garden, La Chaire, dated January 2003 and written by Tony Russell. The Whortleberry Vaccinium myrtillus grows wild on the Quantock Hills and is known regionally by different names. It is perfect for jam making or baked tarts

46 The quote was taken from a press release entitled 'The Samuel Curtis Garden, La Chaire', dated January 2003 and written by Tony Russell

47 Linnaean Society Proceedings, xxii-xxiii, 1855-61

48 The plant Eugenia ugni is also known as Chilean guava and botanically as *Myrtus ugni*

49 Kew Archive. DC (37) English Letters (1857) f.86

50 Kew Archive. DC (33) English Letters (1853) f.99

51 Kew Archive. DC (33) English Letters (1853) f.99

52 Kew Archive. DC (37) English Letters (1857) f.86

53 Kew Archive. DC (37) English Letters (1857) f.86